PRISM SERIES
VOL. 10

Differentiating Instruction in the Inclusive Classroom

STRATEGIES FOR

SUCCESS

BARBARA C. GARTIN
NIKKI L. MURDICK
DARLENE E. PERNER
MARCIA B. IMBEAU

Council for
Exceptional
Children

DADD
*Division on Autism and
Developmental Disabilities*

Council for Exceptional Children
2900 Crystal Drive, Suite 1000
Arlington, VA 22202-3557
www.cec.sped.org

Library of Congress Cataloging-in-Publication data

Gartin, Barbara C. Differentiating instruction in the inclusive classroom: Strategies for success. Prism Series Volume 10 / Barbara C. Gartin, Nikki L. Murdick, Darlene E. Perner, and Marcia B. Imbeau. p. cm. Includes biographical references.

ISBN 978-0-86586-513-6 (soft cover)
ISBN 978-0-86586-514-3 (eBook)

Stock No. P6180

Cover by Wendy Brewer, DesignBox Graphics
Design by Tom Karabatakis, Tompromo Marketing

Printed in the United States of America by United Graphics, LLC

First edition

10 9 8 7 6 5 4 3 2 1

FSC
www.fsc.org
MIX
Paper from
responsible sources
FSC® C102027

Contents

About the Authors 1

Foreword *by Carol Ann Tomlinson* 3

Chapter 1
What Is Differentiated Instruction? 7

Chapter 2
How Does a Teacher Differentiate Instruction? 13

Chapter 3
How Does a Teacher Develop a Healthy Learning Environment? 25

Chapter 4
How Does a Teacher Modify Content? 33

Chapter 5
How Does a Teacher Change the Learning Process? 41

Chapter 6
How Does a Teacher Modify the Product? 49

Chapter 7
What Does Differentiated Instruction in an Inclusive Classroom Look Like? 55

References 73

About the Authors

Barbara C. Gartin
University Professor of Special Education Emeritus
University of Arkansas
bgartin@uark.edu

Nikki L. Murdick
Professor of Special Education
Graduate Program Director, Special Education, Curriculum and Instruction, & Educational Foundations
Saint Louis University
murdickn@slu.edu

Darlene E. Perner
Professor and Chairperson
Department of Exceptionality Programs
Bloomsburg University of Pennsylvania
dperner@bloomu.edu

Marcia B. Imbeau
Professor, Department of Curriculum and Instruction
University of Arkansas
mimbeau@uark.edu

Foreword

During my years as a middle school teacher, my classroom was next door to a colleague who taught students with significant cognitive—and sometimes physical—challenges. My colleague and I created opportunities for our students to work together, and I was repeatedly moved by the evident pleasure the students exhibited when they shared a task or saw one another in the halls or in the cafeteria. I was talking with Joe one day as he was leaving my class. He stopped what he was saying in mid-sentence to greet Philip, a student from our neighbor classroom. Joe slapped Philip on the shoulder and said, "It's good to see you, friend." "Me too," Philip said with a smile that covered his face.

Joe spun back around to resume our conversation and said, "I'm glad we've become friends with the kids next door." "Can you tell me why that's important to you?" I asked. He paused just briefly, nodded, and said, "I think we need each other. I help him with his numbers. He makes me laugh. And I think we teach each other how to be human."

Before my colleague and I connected (and later connected our students), I struggled with the "separateness" of my adolescent neighbors. Our proximity, combined with the distance between the school world of my students and the school world of the students next door, felt awkward to me—alienating. We were silent in one another's presence, as though we couldn't see one another, or as though we spoke in different tongues. Like Joe, I was glad when we became friends. It was easy when we were together, as though we belonged in the same space.

Those were days before inclusion was in the educational lexicon. My teacher-friend and I saw immediate and expanding benefits to the bridge we built between our classrooms, and between the experiences of our students. It never occurred to us (at least in a way we could verbalize) that the bridge was little more than a nod in the direction we needed to go. We never found the words to say to one another that, in fact, our students did belong in the same space—that there was an unnecessary loneliness in the coming and going between our rooms—that her students were still isolated from much of middle school life—that mine were isolated, too, from people who would have extended their experiences as well.

Since those days, as educational practice has evolved, as I moved to a university setting, and as I have had the chance to visit classrooms in which inclusion is both natural and effective, I have added powerful images to my sense of what it can be like—what it ought to be like—when a broad spectrum of young people learn together with leadership from educators who learn how to accentuate human similarities while addressing learning differences.

I spent considerable time in an elementary school in Missouri where I am pretty sure every class had students with significant cognitive or physical challenges. In each instance, those students were as fully integrated into the fabric of the classroom as any other student. There seemed to be no barriers to friendships or to working partnerships. It occurred to me one day that I couldn't recall having been in a school where I had seen such a large number of students with visible learning challenges, so I asked the principal if my observation was correct and why that might be the case. I should have known the answer before she spoke. Parents in that geographic area learned quickly that in this school, their children with complex learning needs would fully belong, so they eagerly moved into the neighborhood.

In a middle school class, I watched an English teacher and a social studies teacher who teamed with each another, with a special educator, and with a teacher of students for whom English was not a first language. The two general educators taught thematically so that there were continual connections between the content of the two courses and between the content of the two courses and the students' lives. Because the teachers taught in rooms next door to one another and in a 2-hour block, they could move students from room to room, and they could move as well. Teachers and students alike worked in varied configurations from day to day and even within a day. There was time to learn, plan, and think as a whole and time to work on what individuals or small groups of students needed to work on as well. All four teachers worked with all of the students. It was a well-choreographed dance—artful, purposeful, satisfying.

I visited a high school math class for only a single class period. It was the day before a major test and the teacher began by taking questions from students about the review work and homework they had been doing. She reminded them that there were two primary operations they would need to employ on the test, and she provided them with three options during the current class. Students who felt a particular need for additional practice and support with the first operation could go to the front right of the room. Those who felt it more important to have practice and support with the second operation could go to the back right of the classroom. Those who wanted practice and support with both operations could go to the center left of the classroom. It was at that point that I realized there were two teachers in the room. The teacher who had begun the class worked with one group of students. The second teacher moved back and forth between the second and third groups. I never could tell which teacher was the "real" math teacher and which was the special educator. I also could never tell which students had identified special education needs. And I tried!

As the authors of this book note, there will likely always be some students for whom a special class is an imperative for some—or even all—of a day, year, or school career. In those instances, differentiation is nearly always a given for a teacher who works with a small group of students whose needs are as variable as in classes three or four times their size. Those teachers learn to teach flexibly because there is no other way to serve their students.

It is the goal of differentiation, as I understand it, to provide a framework for instructional planning that makes room in the classroom for the broadest possible range of learners—for them to sit together, work together, learn together, and be human together. We live in a world and in a time where it is easy to feel separate, isolated, unaccepted, closed-off, and ultimately resentful, angry, and alienated. There is no better antidote for that condition than thousands of classrooms in thousands of schools across the world whose teachers say to their students every day—in word and in action—"We are stronger and better together than we are apart. There is a place for you to be successful in this classroom. We are a team and we can work together to become a winning team."

That is the goal of this book, which simply and straightforwardly lays out a way for teachers at any point in their careers to make sense of, plan for, and enact truly inclusive classrooms. This book is written by educators who have spent much of their professional life teaching and modeling inclusion, both in public schools and at the university level. In the hands of other caring and determined teachers, this is a worthy tool!

Carol Ann Tomlinson
William Clay Parrish, Jr. Professor
Chair, Educational Leadership, Foundations and Policy
Curry School of Education
University of Virginia

CHAPTER 1

What Is Differentiated Instruction?

In the 21st-century classroom, teachers face a student body that is culturally, economically, and linguistically diverse, with disparate needs and abilities—even though many parents, teachers, and administrators still believe in the "myth of homogeneity by virtue of chronological age" (Tomlinson et al., 2003, p. 119). As diversity increases, grouping students by chronological age only despite such factors as readiness or ability continues to be an increasingly questionable practice. Diversities that must be addressed in today's schools include not only the issues of student readiness, language and culture, and ability/disability, but also student interests and individual learning profiles (Hoover & Patton, 2004). Today's educational professionals are seeking a means of addressing this diversity in the classroom through an approach to teaching that is responsive to all the learners they serve. Lachat noted, "Diversity in today's classrooms and schools continues to increase. Classrooms now consist of students who represent many different cultures, languages, and beliefs" (as cited in Hoover, 2009, p. 5). Hoover (2009) went on to add that "Valuing cultural diversity is imperative if diverse learners are to be effectively educated" (Hoover, 2009, p. 5). One way educators are addressing this challenge is through the use of differentiated instruction in the general education classroom (Bender, 2012; Fogarty & Pete, 2011; Gartin, Murdick, Imbeau, & Perner, 2002; Gould & Vaughn, 2000; Gregory, 2003; Hanson, 2015; Hoover, 2009; Hoover & Patton, 2004; Tomlinson, 2014; Tomlinson et al., 2003; Tomlinson & Imbeau, 2010; Tomlinson & McTighe, 2006).

Differentiated instruction was originally defined as the planning of curriculum and instruction using strategies that address student strengths, interests, skills, and readiness in flexible learning environments (Gartin et al., 2002). Tomlinson (2000) suggested that differentiated instruction is "a way of thinking about teaching and learning" (p. 6). Gregory (2003) agreed and noted that "it is a philosophy that enables teachers to plan strategically in order to reach the needs of the diverse learner in classrooms today" (p. 27). Thus, differentiated instruction is an approach to education that holds that:

- Students differ in their readiness to learn.
- Students differ in their readiness, significantly enough to affect their learning.
- Students learn best with high expectations and support from adults.
- Students learn best when material is connected to their interests and experiences.
- Students learn best in a safe community.
- Schools must maximize every student's capacity.

These beliefs continue to serve as guiding principles to direct the actions of teachers today. Osborne noted that "differentiated instruction is an approach to more effectually address the needs of a wide range of learners by providing 'multiple pathways' in the teaching and learning process" (as cited in Bennett, 2012). For the purposes of this book, differentiated instruction will be considered "a way of thinking about teaching and learning" that is "designed to assist teachers in recognizing, understanding, and addressing student differences that are inevitable in virtually all classrooms" (Tomlinson & Imbeau, 2013, p. 120).

Underpinnings of Differentiation of Instruction

Since Tomlinson's (1999) introduction of the concept of differentiated instruction, there have been numerous publications describing it and explaining how to implement it in the inclusive classroom (see Bender, 2012; Fogarty & Pete, 2011; Gartin et al., 2002; Gould & Vaughn, 2000; Gregory, 2003; Hanson, 2015; Hoover, 2009; Hoover & Patton, 2004; Tomlinson et al., 2003; Tomlinson, 2014; Tomlinson & Imbeau, 2010; Tomlinson & McTighe, 2006). In addition to these descriptive articles and books, there has been a surge in research supporting the concept. The major lines of research that provide an underpinning for the concept and implementation of differentiated instruction focus on the concepts of universal design for learning (UDL) and multiple intelligences, informed by recent research in the field of neuroscience.

Universal Design for Learning

The concept of UDL was first developed as a framework to promote flexible instructional environments and to increase access to the educational arena for individuals with disabilities. It was an extension of the concept of universal design, which first began more than 25 years ago in the field of architecture. The Center for Applied Special Education Technology (CAST) focuses the UDL framework on three guiding principles: (a) multiple means of representation, (b) multiple means of expression, and (c) multiple means of engagement (Hanson, 2015). Kame'enui and Simmons (1999) explained the use of universal design through six curricular design principles that are essential for teachers to consider when designing adaptations of content:

- big ideas,
- conspicuous strategies,
- mediated scaffolding,
- strategic integration,
- judicious review, and
- primed background knowledge.

The research base in this area is limited but growing, so teachers interested in the implementation of UDL and differentiated instruction should pay attention to what is happening in the field. Also, according to Janney and Snell (2013), UDL along with differentiated instruction should not be regarded as specific methods or strategies for teachers to use but rather as broad approaches to assist the teacher in responding to student variability in a more focused manner.

Multiple Intelligences

Another area of research that complements the concept of differentiated instruction is that of multiple intelligences. Research on the idea that student learning differences are based on different forms of intelligence was first introduced by Howard Gardner (1993). Gardner proposed the idea that intelligence was not a single ability that could be assessed and that, rather, there were seven—later amended to nine—different forms of intelligence: linguistic, logical-mathematical, spatial, bodily-kinesthetic, musical, interpersonal, intrapersonal, naturalistic, and existential (Bender, 2012). This theory led to research and teaching that focused on including an array of different teaching methods in the classroom. Other theories that address different forms of intelligence as well as learning styles have been proposed (cf. Silver, Strong, & Perini, 2000; Sternberg, 1985). Each of these theories has expanded the concept that students learn in different ways and have preferences for both taking in information and showing what they have learned. Thus, differentiated instruction, which focuses on student differences in learning and processing information, is compatible with the theory of multiple intelligences. Teachers, whether they espouse the theory of multiple intelligences or the theory of differentiated instruction, should plan and develop activities that align with the differing learner strengths, needs and preferences in the classroom.

Brain Research

A new and rapidly expanding area of research has occurred in neuroscience, specifically including research on the brain, brain-compatible learning, and its implications for education. One early focus was that of the active learning brain. Early research by Hart (1999) and Jensen (1998, 2005) introduced the idea that individuals learn better when they are actively involved in the learning process. CAST, in its focus on UDL, has incorporated this research into its pantheon. CAST has described different brain networks that can influence learning and should be considered when designing instruction (see CAST, 2015). These networks include the *recognition network* (what the student is learning), the *strategic network* (how the student is learning), and the *affective network* (why the student is learning; Hanson, 2015). This expanding neuroscience base, now known as *educational neuroscience*, supports the use of differentiating curriculum and instruction in the areas of content, process, product, and the learning environment itself (Sousa & Tomlinson, 2011; also see Chapter 5).

The Future of Differentiated Instruction

Differentiation of instruction is an effective concept for addressing the diverse needs in the 21st-century classroom, and a concept for which there is an expanding research base. Challenges inherent in the inclusive, diverse classrooms of today can be met through implementing the concept of differentiated instruction. Although early application of differentiated instruction activities focused on children who were gifted and talented, more recent application has used differentiated instruction strategies within the general education classroom to enhance the effectiveness of instruction for all students, including those with learning and behavioral disabilities. Students with varying academic readiness, interests, and learning profiles, including students with severe learning and behavioral disabilities, are now being included in general education classrooms. Differentiated instruction offers teachers in today's general education classrooms strategies to support the needs of an increasingly diverse student body. Differentiated instruction has become a "catch word" for curricular development for teachers in general education classrooms because it has proven effective in preparing curriculum and instruction to meet the needs of all learners.

As research on the concept of differentiating instruction continues to develop, there will be additional factors to consider. Will computer-based instructional presentations and social networking opportunities affect the development or implementation of differentiated instruction? What will be the result of the increased focus on response-to-intervention initiatives and the emphasis on addressing individual student needs (Bender & Waller, 2011)? How will the requirement for focusing lesson content and assessment of student progress on common standards (whether the Common Core or state standards) influence the use of differentiated instruction in classrooms of the future? Although there may be additional questions that will arise for teachers, the range of academic diversity most teachers will encounter will likely continue to increase. The aim of differentiated instruction is to provide a strategy to enable teachers to address the needs of all learners including those who are identified or not with learning and behavioral disabilities.

CHAPTER 2

How Does a Teacher Differentiate Instruction?

In order to effectively differentiate instruction, it is essential to understand the concept of curriculum and how it differs from the concept of instruction. According to Oliva and Gordon (2013), the word *curriculum* "can be conceived in a narrow way (as subjects taught) or in a broad way (as all the experiences of learners, both in school and out, directed by the school)" (p. 4). When educators are faced with developing and implementing instruction for students with varying abilities, this question of how to define the term *curriculum* becomes especially significant. Hoover and Patton (2005) considered curriculum to be "one of the first issues classroom teachers encounter in the overall teaching and learning process" (p. 6). Without having a clear understanding of what constitutes a curriculum and the forms in which it appears, it is often impossible for teachers to adequately design instruction that is effectively differentiated to meet the needs of the students in the classroom as well as to address state or Common Core standards requirements.

Types of Curricula

Curricula can be identified as one of three types: (a) explicit, (b) hidden, or (c) absent (Hoover & Patton, 2005). An *explicit curriculum* is the formal curriculum developed by a school district through its policy development process and provided to the teachers for use in preparing their lessons. This is the curriculum with which teachers are the most familiar; it includes the district's stated goals and objectives for each subject-matter area.

The *hidden curriculum* is the one that the teachers actually teach. According to Hoover and Patton (2005), the hidden curriculum is developed "as teachers make inferences about the explicit curriculum they are required to teach" (p. 7). Decisions as to the length of time subjects are taught, the structure of the classroom, and the activities incorporated into the lesson are examples of the hidden curriculum.

The final type of curriculum is called the *absent curriculum*. As teachers and schools select the content of the explicit and hidden curriculum, a number of topics are typically omitted from that discussion. These omitted items comprise the absent curriculum. Unfortunately, those omitted topics may be just as important as what is actually taught. For example, the internment of Japanese Americans during World War II was not included in American History books for many years following the war. For teachers who are preparing to design differentiated instruction, these different forms of curriculum may present a hindrance in the process. As Tomlinson and Allan (2000) stated, "Teachers sometimes find themselves struggling against a district curriculum that seems more standardized than differentiated. This situation is aggravated if the curriculum is largely a collection of topics, facts, and skills—a difficult kind of curriculum to differentiate" (pp. 90–91). In other words, a curriculum should not be seen as a fixed or immutable entity, but rather as a set of factors working in tandem. In differentiated instruction, teachers focus on what to teach in terms of what they wish students to learn. They describe what they want students to learn in terms of what students will know, understand, and be able to do.

Designing Instruction to Meet Curriculum Standards

Confusion often arises as to the difference and relationship between the concepts of curriculum and instruction. As teachers begin planning instruction, they try to clarify the two interrelated concepts. Oliva and Gordon (2013) provided a clear separation of these two concepts: "decisions about the curriculum relate to plans or programs and thus are *programmatic*, whereas those about instruction (and thereby implementation) are *methodological*" (p. 7). Teachers preparing to design instruction should consider the three types of curricula (i.e., explicit, hidden, absent) with the program to be taught and then design instruction to implement this program using the most appropriate methods by which the learning is to take place.

Therefore, teachers need to design instruction not only to meet the core curriculum standards set forth by their district or state, but also, and more important, to meet the specific instructional needs of students. In other words, teachers should begin their instructional design and development by addressing "two critical 'givens': there are content requirements—often in the form of standards—that will serve as destination points for their students, and there are students who will inevitably vary as learners" (Tomlinson, 2014, p. 3). Thus, in order to design effective instruction that addresses both of these "critical givens," the teacher must begin by answering three basic but essential questions:

- What is the terminal goal of the instructional path?
- How do you plan to get to the terminal goal?
- How will you know when you have reached the goal?

Without considering these three questions, the lessons that are developed may not be clear enough to differentiate for the various learning needs of the students in the classroom. As Tomlinson (1999) noted in her seminal work (*The Differentiated*

Classroom: Responding to the Needs of All Learners), lessons that are unclear or "hazy" do not support differentiated instruction, because

> When a teacher lacks clarity about what a student should know, understand, and be able to do as a result of a lesson, the learning tasks she creates may or may not be engaging and we can almost be certain the tasks won't help students understand essential ideas or principles. A fuzzy sense of the essentials results in fuzzy activities, which, in turn, results in fuzzy student understanding. (p. 37)

The remedy for this ambiguity is to plan a focused curriculum with a clear idea of the relationship between curriculum and instruction. A *focused curriculum* articulates distinct goals concerning what students should know (e.g., facts and vocabulary), understand (e.g., concepts, principles, generalizations), and be able to do (e.g., skills) as a result of the lesson, lesson sequence, unit, or year of instruction. According to Hanson (2015), teachers must also ensure that learners "feel emotionally and physically safe, make connections to experience, engage in active and authentic learning, and receive frequent feedback" (p. 2). In addition, when designing the lesson, teachers must remember to (a) link the lesson to prior and subsequent learning, (b) provide a context for the lesson, (c) choose activities that will advance student understanding, (d) use active lessons to enhance learning, (e) provide authentic practice that uses skills for real situations, and (f) customize the lesson structure and pacing to fit the students' needs (Hanson, 2015). From this information, one should be able to prepare instruction that is of high quality and that also addresses the key elements of a differentiated classroom.

The Essentials of Differentiating Instruction

Differentiated instruction provides a framework for teachers to consider the students in their classrooms, the curriculum to be provided, and the manner in which this information is to be presented. Tomlinson and Imbeau (2013, p. 121) presented a visual model to assist teachers in understanding curriculum and its specific and interrelated components, as a basis for differentiation. In order to design instruction that will respond to student needs, teachers are guided by five general principles of differentiation:

- providing a supportive learning environment,
- presenting a quality curriculum,
- developing assessment that informs teaching and learning,
- designing instruction that responds to student variance, and
- organizing the classroom in a way that allows the teacher to lead and manage learning.

Differentiation of the curriculum and subsequent instruction can be divided into four specific and interrelated components: content, process, product, and learning environment (Janney & Snell, 2013; Tomlinson & Imbeau, 2013). Each of these components must therefore be addressed in anticipation of and response to student differences in readiness, interest, and learning preferences.

Content

Content can be defined as what the student should know, understand, and be able to do as a result of learning. According to Tomlinson (2001), "content is the 'input' of teaching and learning. It's what we teach or what we want students to learn" (p. 72). In other words, this is what the teacher plans to teach based on the school, district, or state standards as well as the needs of the student.

Process

Process refers to the activities, lessons, and interactions that occur during the school day to help students use their skills to make sense of the content being presented. These activities, lessons, and interactions are the structure that supports and enhances the content. Tomlinson (2001) expanded this idea by saying that any activity, lesson, or interaction "achieves maximum power as a vehicle for learning only when it is squarely focused on a portion of something essential that students need to know, understand, and be able to do" (p. 79).

Product

Products are the planned result(s) of the "sense-making activities" (i.e., the process) that the teacher has designed. The teacher develops the resulting product so that, when completed, it represents the acquired skills that the content and process were designed for the student to learn. Thus, products can be used as an assessment instrument to assure the student has learned the desired curriculum. In other words, products are the means by which the student demonstrates successful acquisition of knowledge after participating in the planned process activities, lessons, or interactions.

Learning Environment

The learning environment includes all facets of the classroom and school, including the physical and emotional contexts where the learning is to occur. Learning environment plays a significant factor in whether students feel comfortable and ready to learn (Tomlinson & Imbeau, 2010). Thus, a review of the learning environment— also known as an *environmental assessment*—should take into consideration the physical outlook and plan of the classroom as well as the school, the number and the type of grouping of students within the classroom, and the physical environment (including heat, light, and noise; see Salend, 2011, for a sample environmental assessment form). Each of these factors affect—either positively or negatively—any curriculum and instruction.

Planning and Implementing Differentiated Instruction

Each of the elements of differentiated instruction (i.e., content, process, product, learning environment) does not stand isolated from the others and is interrelated in practice. When planning to differentiate classroom curriculum and instruction for students with varying abilities, a teacher must consider each of these components separately as well as consider how they interact. To assist in this process, Tomlinson and Allan (2000, pp. 142–143) developed their "Guide for Planning Differentiated Instruction," which uses a question format to support the instructional planning process. The guide poses seven questions to direct a teacher in planning for differentiation. First, teachers should ask themselves if they are clear on what they want the student to know (facts, information), understand (principles, generalizations, ideas), and be able to do (basic skills, skills of the discipline and thinking skills) as a result of this learning experience. Following this essential first step, teachers should decide on the content and consider alternate sources and resources, varied support systems, and varied pacing plans. This might involve accessing web sites or incorporating other technology resources or supports, audio recordings of readings or directions, and timelines that can be adjusted to support student success. Of course, prior to designing any lesson, teachers will need to develop a pre-assessment to determine students' prior knowledge, understandings or skills in order to prepare appropriate content and activities.

Next, teachers should consider the most effective way to group students or tasks so that learning can occur. That is, as teachers assign students to groups or tasks, they must ensure that the following occurs: students in groups vary from previous recent ones, students are encouraged to "work up" (meaning the task causes them to grow, but not drown), provisions are made (if appropriate) for students who need or prefer to work alone, and the chosen group size matches student needs. After deciding how to group students for a particular lesson or unit, teachers can then create differentiated activities. All activities should be designed so that they:

- call for high-level thinking,

- appear equally interesting to learners,

- vary along a difficulty continuum (see Tomlinson, 2014, for a description of her Equalizer Tool for differentiating instruction when addressing students' readiness),

- include student choices of how to apply skills or how to express them,
- provide opportunities for varied modes of learning,
- are squarely focused on one (or a few) key concepts and generalizations,
- integrate appropriate skills into activity requirements,
- clearly delineate expectations,
- include a plan for gathering ongoing assessment, and
- identify a plan or mechanism for bringing closure and clarity.

Along with differentiating activities, teachers should create product assignments that vary along a continuum based on student readiness or appeal to different learner preferences. It is important that all student products use key concepts, generalizations, and ideas to solve problems and create meaningful products—and allow students to have a choice in the product they create. As with differentiated activities, it is essential to provide delineated and appropriately challenging expectations for product content; in addition, both student and teacher might be able to add additional criteria for success. Finally, product assignment design should include plans for formative and summative evaluation and a system that allows for family involvement as appropriate.

The final step that teachers need to complete is to think about and select the type of instructional strategies that might be appropriate for helping students meet the learning goals (e.g., contracts, centers, compacting). This selection is based on strategies that will most appropriately delineate the content, the organization of instructional groups that will enhance student learning of the content, the method by which teachers will sample student understanding of the content, and the meaningful tasks for reinforcement, extension, and exploration that teachers will include in their lessons (Tomlinson & Allan, 2000).

Although any teacher can differentiate instruction within a classroom, it may be wise for school leaders to encourage all teachers to consider differentiation a consistent practice of their classrooms. However, before teachers can implement any model of instructional planning, there are a number of essential features that must be discussed with the school administration.

First, the essentials of a plan must be considered along with decisions made as to who will prepare the schoolwide plan, who will implement it, and whether or not these will be the same people. Differentiated instruction often requires time for professional development and time to locate or prepare materials as well as funding to cover costs, so a discussion with school administration must include answers to the questions of who will pay, where materials will be stored, and who has custody of the materials. In addition, a decision should be made as to who will monitor and evaluate the actions taken toward the implementation of the program as well as how and what will be the criteria for success. Answers to such questions must be addressed and possibly negotiated with the school administration. This needs to be done prior to implementation, with all involved parties receiving the information.

After all parties have approved the plan, the actual work begins. Identification of student and class needs must occur. Data need to be collected to determine whether individual students have difficulty accessing the content, storing or remembering the content, or expressing or demonstrating competency. Many schools and districts utilize professional learning communities (PLCs) or grade or department teams as a means for discussing data and specific student issues which may be a good vehicle that is already in place for this element of planning.

One concern that is often posed by teachers is whether modification is the most appropriate way for students to be successful. The implementation of differentiated instruction does not supersede providing intensive instruction in academic and social domains for students who require such instruction—meaning that a teacher might need to consider *what* such students learn (modifications) in addition to *how* they learn it (accommodations). A related concern for some students with developmental disabilities is whether the best location of the instruction is in the general education classroom or in a more specialized setting. The preferred setting for instruction of all students is the general education classroom. This preference was supported in the 2004 amendments to the Individuals With Disabilities Education Act, which stressed that the general education classroom and curriculum is the focal point for the instruction of students with disabilities (34 CFR §300.550[b]). However, decisions concerning the most appropriate educational setting for a student with disabilities ultimately must be based on that student's unique and specific needs as determined by the multidisciplinary team (34 CFR §300.552[a] [1] and [b][1] and [2]).

Finally, it is imperative that anyone who uses a model for differentiated instruction consider the issue of short-term adaptations versus lifelong skill development. The focus of an effective educational plan is to provide students with skills that lead to success in the future. Adaptations through a differentiated instruction curricular model support that goal. Those developing a plan for students with diverse needs must assure that incompetence or dependency is not built into the plan through the instructional adaptations. For example, if a student needed audio recordings of new material to be able to access it because of a reading difficulty, a wise teacher would be careful to build the student's skills and stamina to have him read more familiar material aloud. Eventually, students who have become more proficient in reading might record their reading for evidence of progress or for another child who needs access to the material, fostering competence and independence for both rather than dependency.

A Model for Differentiating Instruction

One model that has been used consistently over the past 2 decades is Schumm, Vaughn, and Leavell's "planning pyramid" (1994). Although Schumm and colleagues developed the planning pyramid as a way to assist teachers in adapting content-area textbooks, their work continues to be invaluable to teachers working with students who are learning material at different speeds, who are functioning at different academic levels, who have varying levels of academic readiness, who have diverse learning preferences, and who have a wide range of interests. According to Gould and Vaughn (2000), Schumm et al.'s model provides a framework for planning for diverse students' needs in an inclusive classroom and is "especially useful in planning content area lessons…where there is great variation in student ability levels" (p. 364). The planning pyramid provides a method for teachers to focus on identifying adaptations as a component of developing a comprehensive plan for students with developmental disabilities. Although this model is designed for use in content-area instruction, it can be used when designing differentiated lessons in the inclusive, diverse classrooms of today.

The planning pyramid (see Figure 2.1; Schumm et al., 1994; see also Schumm, 1999; Gould & Vaughn, 2000) has two primary dimensions: the five points of the pyramid (four at the base and one at the top) and the three vertical levels or tiers. The base of the pyramid has four points: topic, classroom context, teacher, and appropriate instructional practices. The apex of the pyramid, the fifth point, is the student. For each of these points of entry, and before beginning to identify or develop lessons and accompanying adaptations, teachers need to consider the influence a particular factor may have on student learning. Next, teachers should determine what is to be taught and how. The second dimension of the pyramid is its vertical division into three tiers that correspond to degrees of learning. The base or lower tier consists of what all students will learn; the middle tier is what most (but not all) students will learn; and the top tier is what some students will learn. Using the information developed during reflection and the three tiers of the pyramid, objectives for each level can be designed. Content determination is dependent on the specific grade level being taught and the school district curricular guidelines, as well as state and national curriculum standards.

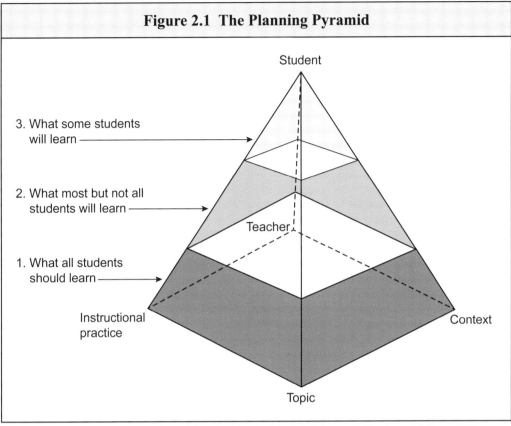

Figure 2.1 The Planning Pyramid

Student

3. What some students
   will learn

2. What most but not all
   students will learn

Teacher

1. What all students
   should learn

Instructional
practice

Context

Topic

Note: Adapted from "Pyramid Power for Collaborative Planning," by J. S. Schumm, S. Vaughn, and J. Harris, 1997, *TEACHING Exceptional Children, 29*(6), p. 63. Copyright 1997 Council for Exceptional Children.

Following this content review, teachers can identify the specific instructional practices and required adaptations to assure that learning occurs for all students. After developing objectives and defining content for students at each of the pyramid levels, the teacher can identify and list appropriate adaptations. This information can be compiled on an instructional planning form (see Figure 2.2).

It is important to note that the majority of intensive adaptations will occur at the base tier, because this level is where all students must learn the information. Teachers who use the instructional planning form can clearly note the essential facets of the lesson. But in order to assure that students with learning and behavioral needs are not relegated to the base tier throughout their school career, modifications must also be presented that will assist them in reaching the middle and even the top tier of the pyramid. According to Schumm (1999), the planning pyramid can be used for individual lessons, weekly lessons, or even unit plans or theme cycles. This structure provides teachers with a planning format as well as a means of communicating with parents and other professionals about individual student instructional goals in comparison with others in the class.

Figure 2.2 Instructional Planning Form

Date:		Period:		Subject:	
Goal:					
Materials required:					
Content	Anticipatory set	Learning activity	Rehearsal activity	Learning activity	Evaluation activity
What *some* students will learn					
What *most* students will learn					
What *all* students should learn					
Adaptations	Anticipatory set	Learning activity	Rehearsal activity	Learning activity	Evaluation activity
Content					
Product					
Process					
Environment					

Differentiation in the Inclusive Classroom

Curriculum typically is established long before the students enter the school. A curriculum represents what society values as important so that students can become productive citizens and successful individuals. If a curriculum accurately represents what is considered important knowledge within society, then it should have the potential to provide all students the opportunity to acquire this knowledge and accompanying skills. However, to accommodate students with diverse needs, it may be necessary to prioritize the content to ensure that the most important content is mastered (i.e., what all need to know). Teachers should teach so that all students obtain an understanding and mastery of the most critical content.

After determining what all students should learn, content must be organized and sequenced. Unit objectives must be determined, and instructional objectives must be defined. A task analysis of the concept being taught might be helpful because the content of the lesson is reduced into several smaller, simpler, and easier-to-learn tasks. To assist in student learning, the teacher should then select exemplars and non-exemplars of the concept (e.g., if you are helping students come to see the concept of patterns in numbers you might show students the even numbers 2, 4, 6 as an exemplar and a sequence of random numbers as a non-exemplar). In support of the content, the teacher will need to select books, materials, and additional resources that address a wide array of reading levels, interests, and input modalities. Presentations, evaluations, and activities must be planned and diverse teaching materials must be obtained or developed. All of the previously stated decisions provide the framework for structuring instruction so that it is more likely to meet the needs of all the students in the classroom. The richer the resources available to the teacher, the greater the possibility of meeting the diverse needs of students within the inclusive classroom.

When the decision to implement differentiated instruction in a diverse classroom is made, perhaps the first issue that must be addressed is the curriculum. Without a clear understanding of the district's explicit standardized curriculum and how it differs from the hidden curriculum (i.e., what is actually taught in the classroom), it becomes difficult to adequately design differentiated lessons for successful learning. Tomlinson (1999, 2001, 2014) suggested that curricula includes clearly defined learning goals stated as what students should know, understand, and be able to do. How teachers help all students reach those learning goals involves strategic planning regarding content (what students are to learn or how they can access it), process (how they come to learn or make sense of the content), product (how students show what they have learned), and learning environment (with special attention to any element that might make the classroom more comfortable and inviting for a student). Although these elements may be addressed individually, they are fundamentally interrelated. The Planning Pyramid (Gould & Vaughn, 2000; Schumm, 1999; Schumm et al., 1994) provides an effective structure to incorporate these elements when planning for differentiated instruction. In the next four chapters, the specific elements of differentiated instruction (learning environment, content, process, and product) will be reviewed to better prepare the teacher of diverse students, including those with developmental disabilities, in inclusive classrooms to address their unique learning needs.

CHAPTER 3

How Does a Teacher Develop a Healthy Learning Environment?

Creating a learning environment that fosters respect, encouragement, acceptance, and joy is the goal of every inclusive classroom. A learning environment such as this emphasizes that all students are respected and that all student work is important and valued. The teacher sets the tone of the classroom; the teacher's attitudes, enthusiasm, and expectations influence the feelings and perceptions of students concerning themselves and others. What are the characteristics of a healthy inclusive classroom and how does a teacher design the classroom environment to support learning for all?

Implementing a philosophy of inclusion and differentiation requires that teachers address the learning needs of their students while making significant changes to instruction and the instructional learning environment (i.e., the classroom). This approach to teaching means that when implementing the concept of inclusion and differentiation, teacher roles and responsibilities also must change (Janney & Snell, 2013). A primary responsibility of a teacher in an inclusive classroom who is implementing differentiation is to be intentional about several elements of the learning environment that enhance student and teacher success. Three major components of healthy learning environments are classroom physical arrangements, instructional groupings, and classroom climate. Classroom climate, in particular, has been identified as a strong predictor of student success (Dweck, 2000; Hamre et al., 2012; Hattie, 2009).

Classroom Physical Arrangement

When assessing the physical environment where the community of learners will work and play every day, the teacher should consider different aspects of the classroom, including: access to other students and staff, adequacy of the space for the form of learning that will occur, physical access issues in the room and building that might impact student mobility, availability of distraction-free or reduced-distraction areas, and ease of access to technology and manipulative materials (see Table 3.1). Decisions based on this environmental assessment are especially important in an inclusive classroom incorporating differentiated instruction. In addition, the teacher should consider the number of students in the class, the behavioral and academic issues of the students, and the types of learning activities that may be used (Bender, 2012). Creating a climate where everyone has access to the teacher and the materials is essential for student success.

The physical layout of a classroom is often a reflection of the teacher's style of teaching. However, in the inclusive classroom, the focus is on addressing the needs of both teacher and students. How can the classroom's physical arrangement be modified to support student learning? One way to modify a classroom environment is through the arrangement of its furniture. During the instructional day, teachers may need to allow time for students to move desks or tables to better fit the activities occurring in class. For example, if the instructional activities are teacher-directed, then placing the teacher's desk in the front of the room is appropriate; but if the activity is a group discussion with the teacher as facilitator, then abandoning the desk to sit in a student desk within a large circle might be more appropriate. Nunley (2006) also suggested adding one or more tables to the room to encourage collaborative learning. If the classroom space does not permit the use of a table, then desks can be moved together facing each other to form a table-like surface. In some instances, teachers may need to think beyond their classrooms and look for an empty classroom nearby that can be used as a quiet area if one is needed. It is essential for the teacher to provide a room arrangement that is flexible enough to employ a variety of different instructional strategies (Bartlett, Weisenstein, & Etscheidt, 2002; Bos & Vaughn, 2015; Janney & Snell, 2013; Nunley, 2006).

Whatever the classroom arrangement, teachers should remember that the goal is to assist in addressing the varying learning needs of the students in the classroom. Teachers may provide easily distracted students with some privacy through the addition of desktop privacy shields, a study carrel, or private office within the classroom; these students may benefit from having their desks positioned away from distracters such as doors and windows, out of high-traffic areas, or in quieter areas of the classroom. Other students who require redirection may need to be seated near the teacher's desk, near the chalkboard, or close to (or far from) particular peers. However, it is important to remember that classroom arrangement and individual student positioning should not result in students feeling isolated or separated from others in the room. If it does, the goal of classroom cohesion and positive climate will be lost (Janney & Snell, 2013; Miller, 2002; Nunley, 2006, Tomlinson & Imbeau, 2010).

Table 3.1 Learning Environment Checklist		
Component	**Does it allow/include….**	
Seating		Quiet places (study carrels, loner seats, reading corners, headphone area, and conference area)
		Flexible seating arrangements and grouping
		Multiple-use areas (group work area, tutorial stations, workstation area with easy access to materials)
Classroom organization		Well-established daily routines
		Clear rules with consistent enforcement
		Multiple signals and cues to prepare students for changes in activity
		Student assignments given orally, posted on the board, and written in assignment workbooks
		Easy access to manipulatives and materials
		Easy access storage for wheelchair or crutches
		Aisles that allow students easy movement around the classroom
		Clutter-free spaces that reinforce organization of materials and work practices
Positive climate		Well-established behavioral expectations that have been taught, reinforced regularly, and posted
		Prevention of difficulties through teaching appropriate behaviors
		Posted reminders that are used in praise and correction
		Use of physical proximity and touch to help students re-focus
		Reduction or elimination of textures, sounds, and smells that might be disconcerting to some learners
		Individual positive attention to each student that promotes actions that tell students that they are valued, able, and trusted
		Development of independent thought and action in each student
		Acceptance and valuing of diversity in people and thought
		Love and joy in teaching and learning

Instructional Grouping

One important concept in differentiating instruction is the use of *flexible grouping*, which provides each student with the opportunity to work with a number of peers within a defined period of time (Tomlinson & Imbeau, 2013). Instructional grouping arrangements include large-group instruction, small-group instruction, one-to-one instruction, independent learning activities, cooperative learning groups, and peer-teaching pairs. Because students need to be a part of many different groups, teachers in inclusive classrooms use all different forms of grouping to support successful learning. Sometimes students might select their own group membership, whereas for other activities the teacher might assign group membership. In each case, however, group membership should be flexible and changing so as to allow students to work with a diversity of peers and to prevent any students from being labeled based solely on their group membership. This flexible group membership also prevents some students from always being labeled the "helper" and others as always being labeled the "helped," and it should prevent segregation within the classroom (Nunley, 2006). Regardless of the kind of grouping a teacher would choose to use, the groups should always be used to help students reach the learning goals while also enacting a positive supportive learning environment. Additionally, because the groupings include a variety of arrangements, this element of classroom life signals to everyone an important idea that working with different classmates in many configurations is the norm in this place (Tomlinson & Imbeau, 2010).

Classroom Climate

In addition to the physical arrangement and instructional grouping, the bonding or social interconnectedness of the teacher(s) and students in the class is equally important in providing a healthy classroom climate. Over a decade ago, in her seminal work, Tomlinson (1999) proposed several characteristics of teaching and learning in healthy classroom environments—and recently updated this work maintaining most of the original elements (Tomlinson, 2014, pp. 53–59). These components support the development of a classroom climate that is both conducive to learning and to high achievement for all students, with or without exceptional needs, and include:

- The teacher appreciates each child as an individual.
- The teacher remembers to teach whole children.
- The teacher continues to develop expertise.
- The teacher links students and ideas.
- The teacher strives for joyful learning.

- The teacher offers high expectations and lots of ladders.
- The teacher helps students make their own sense of ideas.
- The teacher shares the teaching with students.
- The teacher clearly strives for student independence.
- The teacher exercises positive classroom management.

Teachers need to have high expectations accompanied by a belief in the ability of all students to learn. Likewise, valuing different abilities and modeling tolerance for such differences are ways of including students with disabilities as well as leading others to recognize their unique abilities. In fact, the teacher must be involved with all the students, not isolated from them. A teacher can demonstrate involvement by consistently working with different groups, by highlighting an individual's accomplishment to the whole class so that all students can celebrate that child's success, or by offering different working arrangements to students so they have choice in how they complete a task. Thus, an inclusive classroom focuses on the best for—and from—each student. These are essential teacher beliefs if the classroom climate is to be conducive to student learning.

All students need individualized attention from the teacher in order to feel that they are essential members of the classroom, so it is important to build in student–teacher one-on-one time into the classroom day. From the moment students enter the classroom, they should feel welcomed. Every student should be greeted by the teacher, and during the day the teacher should engage positively with each individual student. Teachers must implement multiple opportunities for each student to succeed and then recognize and celebrate successes.

It is important that all students feel accepted and valued—not only by the teacher but also their peers. For students with disabilities, it is imperative that teachers identify areas of concern within the classroom milieu and modify the classroom environment so that all students experience a supportive classroom environment.

Social interactions support and assist in the enhancement of relationships between students, both with and without disabilities, and their teachers. One method that can be used to create a more positive classroom environment is peer networks. Peer networks are "groups of individuals who demonstrate an interest in and an understanding of the individual with a disability and have an impact on that person's life" (Bartlett et al., 2002, p. 305). An example of a peer network is Circle of Friends (Forest & Lusthaus, 1989; visit http://www.circleofriends.org), which has been especially useful with students with developmental disabilities. Another example, peer-assisted learning strategies (see http://kc.vanderbilt.edu/pals/about.html), are a highly structured tutoring system successfully used with differentiated instruction (Bender, 2012).

Establishing rituals and traditions can help develop a classroom climate that is inclusive and comfortable for all students (as well as the teacher). For example, the class might develop class rules, a class creed, or a class motto that can be posted on the classroom wall and revisited daily (see Figure 3.1). Refer to the motto when students demonstrate the meaning of the motto and, likewise, refer to it when students are not following its intent or meaning. Remember, the teacher is the main facilitator in building a sense of community, safety, and tolerance in the classroom.

Figure 3.1 Sample Classroom Rules

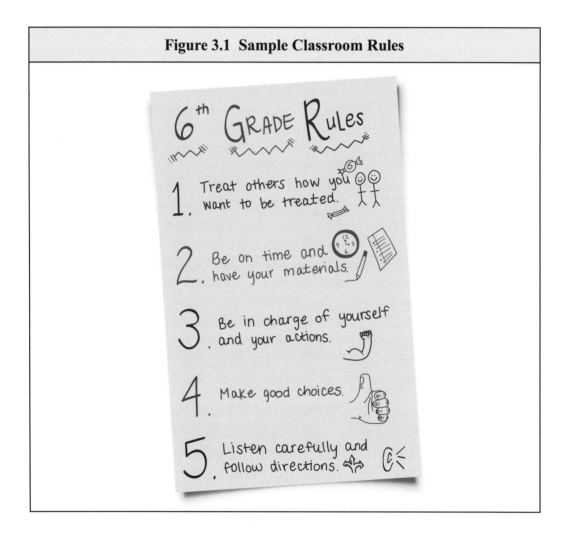

Figure 3.1 Sample Classroom Rules (cont'd)

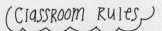

Note. Reprinted from *The Survival Guide for New Special Education Teachers*, by C. Martin and C. Hauth, 2015, p. 47. Copyright 2015 Council for Exceptional Children.

Miller (2002) stated that "organizing the learning environment is a critical component of successful teaching and learning. Even the best content, taught with appropriate learning processes in mind, will be unsuccessful if the classroom environment is not conducive to learning" (p. 82). For students with disabilities to have success in the inclusive classroom, teachers must be prepared to be flexible. Considering different ways of organizing the physical environment, modifying instructional groups, and establishing a positive learning environment increases the possibility of success for all students.

CHAPTER 4

How Does a Teacher Modify Content?

*C*ontent modifications* are changes to instructional curricula or materials to support student learning. General education teachers have long made a practice of modifying instructional materials for students with disabilities or other students considered at risk for school failure. In many cases, modifications that teachers have used in the past are still appropriate for inclusive classrooms. However, the primary differences between past practices and contemporary inclusive education practices are the regularity and purposes surrounding these modifications.

For example, teachers may be accustomed to reducing the number of vocabulary words, reducing the complexity of the definitions, or providing word lists for a student with a learning disability or intellectual disability. In the past, teachers have made these types of modifications on an as-needed basis—not as a regular component in planning instruction for all students in the class. In order for substantive student learning to be achieved, teachers in inclusive classes regularly review learner needs and then adjust the degree and kind of content modification to support all students. Both curricular and instructional modifications are considered content modifications, and may include text alteration, study guides, learning contracts, and activity stations.

Curricular Modifications and Adaptations

In her seminal work, Tomlinson (1999) stressed that what is taught and learned must have student relevance, enhance self-understanding, be authentic, have immediate usability, and enhance student empowerment in the present as well as the future. In 2014, Tomlinson presented the concept of *quality curriculum*, which she described as curriculum that provides student access to rich, engaging content that allows students to assume the roles of thinker and problem solver (p. 64). To accomplish this, the teacher must design content that clearly identifies what students should know, understand, and do. Tomlinson's suggestions concerning curriculum and content are relevant for all students and are especially important for students with disabilities where an appropriate curriculum must be future-focused, functional, and reflective of the general curriculum.

How can curricular decisions be modified to support learning for students with disabilities? According to Janney and Snell (2013), both curriculum and instruction can be adapted so that students can participate in the general education curriculum. For some students with mild or moderate disabilities to be included with their same-age peers, only the content of the curriculum may need adaptation. For those students with more severe disabilities, both the curriculum and the instructional strategies may need to be changed. Janney and Snell (2013) described three types of modified curricula: supplementary curricula, alternative curricula, and simplified curricula.

Supplementary Curricula

One way to adapt the general curriculum to meet students' learning needs is to develop a supplementary curriculum. A *supplementary curriculum* is one in which additional lessons are included to assist in students learning the presented material. For example, teachers develop a supplementary curriculum when they pre-teach the content vocabulary for a unit on a specific topic such as Folktales for elementary learners or The Gulf War for secondary students.

Similarly, when teaching multiplication, teachers often introduce students to the array model. An array is formed by arranging a set of objects into rows and columns, with each column having the same number of objects as the other rows. Before teaching multiplication using arrays, the teacher reviews with students how to decompose, or break down, numbers into numbers more accessible to them. For example, if students are asked to find the product of 13×5, they might decompose 13 into 10 and 3 and then multiply 10×5 and 3×5. Thus, when students are decomposing numbers into arrays, they will have had a refresher in what it means to decompose numbers.

For students who need support in developing noncognitive skills, teachers can incorporate into the curriculum opportunities for social skills or study skills to be introduced or reinforced within the school setting. For example, study skills may be added to the class curriculum by helping all students keep binders of ongoing work, including copies of instructions, guidelines, and rubrics (a *study skills notebook*). During class, teachers can routinely model appropriate ways to ask for clarification, respond to questions, and disagree respectfully. In addition, posted charts can provide visual reminders of the social skills and study skills used by academically successful students. In this way, the curriculum can be expanded with added information or skill development for students who need additional challenges.

All content areas offer opportunities for expanding the curriculum. In a science unit when most students are using a microscope to learn about single-celled organisms by viewing slides of algae, a few students are also taught the parts of a microscope and its function. In this case, the supplemental curriculum includes each individual part and its functionality in the use of a microscope.

Alternative Curricula

An *alternative curriculum* is designed for students who are unable to access the core general education curriculum without significant modifications. In some instances, the needs of the student require the development of an alternative curriculum—that is, a new curriculum is developed in lieu of the original. When the content, process, and product for a student cannot be successfully differentiated, it may be that an alternative curriculum needs to be developed to partially or completely replace the general curriculum. An alternative curriculum often is designed for students with moderate or severe disabilities and is structured in a format depending on the specific student's needs. Skills are taught by direct instruction with extensive support over multiple settings with significant adaptations and modifications. Academic skills, such as measuring within the cooking context, are often below age expectations and might be made a part of the student's daily routine.

Simplified Curricula

A *simplified curriculum* can be considered an "abridged version" of the general curriculum; in other words, the essential components of the curriculum remain, but additional and nonessential materials are omitted. This modification allows students to have the same instructional objectives as their same-age, grade-level peers, but the scope of the curriculum—including skills and concepts—is reduced, condensed, or abbreviated (Janney & Snell, 2013). In simplifying curricula, teachers may adapt both the level of difficulty and the means by which information is provided (Janney & Snell, 2013; see Table 4.1).

There are numerous research-validated strategies that improve content delivery in classrooms, thus increasing the likelihood that students with disabilities will engage with the content. In adapting or modifying content to meet students' needs, teachers can:

- Provide content on the student's level.
- Use assistive technology with all students who might benefit.
- Read materials aloud to class.
- Provide audio recordings of texts, handouts, and instructions to students.
- Incorporate content review and recall activities within the main activity.
- Use the think-pair-share strategy to include all students (see Simon, n.d.).

- Use content cues.
- Use visual displays.
- Develop study guides.
- Use lecture-pause procedures, concept teaching routines, peer tutoring, co-operative learning, and computer-based instruction to help retain and recall content.
- Use authentic content (i.e., topics that are made relevant to students' lives).

Table 4.1 Content and Instructional Adaptations	
Content adaptations	Instructional adaptations
Vary instructional methods (e.g., develop controlled vocabulary or pre-teach vocabulary).	Provide students with outlines or lecture notes beforehand.
Omit extraneous details.	Read material aloud, or have students use text-to-speech readers.
Reduce reading level of text passages or test directions.	Accompany lectures with visual materials (e.g., overheads, graphic organizers, interactive whiteboards, maps).
Provide cues, prompts, and feedback during practice activities.	Provide accompanying audio or video recordings (teacher-made or commercial).
Present "mini-lectures" at 10-minute intervals.	Highlight the essential facts in the text or handouts.
Develop chapter study guides for key concepts and vocabulary terms.	Use hands-on activities.
Use signals (thumbs up or down) or choral responses for comprehension checking.	Include demonstrations of assignments.
Chunk content into small segments.	Provide a physical or online notebook that includes a class calendar, homework assignments, class notes (including those from classroom smartboards), visual materials (e.g., graphic organizers, maps, overheads), study guides, and how-to-do lists.

Multilevel Instruction

Multilevel instruction is an approach that engages all students in the same curricular areas but with differing instructional objectives and varying academic levels. Although multilevel instruction is usually considered a way of differentiating the process of instruction, it is also useful when addressing content differentiation. According to Bartlett et al. (2002), "this strategy has been effective … because it focuses on developing concepts by using content as a means for teaching specific skills, rather than teaching the content as an end in itself" (p. 304). Teachers using multilevel instruction employ a variety of practice activities and teaching strategies—such as curriculum overlapping and tiered assignments—to accommodate the needs of all students in the classroom.

Curriculum overlapping allows students to share an activity while addressing different learning outcomes. This method is useful in embedding functional curriculum skills into the general curriculum. For example, all students learn to estimate, but some students use estimation to determine how much money is needed to go to the movies on a date. *Tiered assignments*, on the other hand, are used to adjust the degree of difficulty of a question, task, or product to match the student's instructional level. To develop a tiered lesson, a teacher first develops clear learning goals (specifying what she wants her students to know, understand, and be able to do). Next, she develops tasks or learning experiences that would be engaging and relevant to students and are carefully aligned to those learning goals but differ in their degree of challenge so that they are likely to fit a range of learner readiness levels. To accompany the multiple versions of the task, the teacher selects supporting materials with levels ranging from basic to advanced. Thus, all students, including those with different degrees of learning proficiency, can be involved in using their skills to learn the content. For example, all students may be studying the same topic in their science class but may be using different sources to acquire some base information that closely matches their skill level in reading. One group of students may be using some Internet sources that are especially good at explaining complex material but at more basic level while others are using more advanced sources. If everyone is using the computer to find, read, or listen to the information, then everyone has access to the content that is a good fit for them.

Instructional Materials to Enhance Student Access to Content

For some students with disabilities, typical classroom texts and other written materials often have a readability level that is too difficult to successfully navigate. Even when students may otherwise be able to understand the content, the reading level of the written material may be a barrier to learning, especially when using content-area textbooks. According to Salend (2011), there are a number of methods by which to adjust readability of material to meet the needs of the students, including modifying content, simplifying the text, and using electronic versions. Salend (2011) also suggested highlighting information in the textbook so that critical information is noted—and highlighting and bookmarking or placing "pins" to mark information is often a feature of electronic textbooks. Picture codes can be used to help identify and rate important materials for the student (e.g., placing symbols in the margin of the text). Key words can be circled or otherwise identified so that their definitions can be learned.

Simplifying materials can be time consuming for teachers, but the strategy has been shown to assist those students with learning difficulties who are included in the general education classroom. Hoover and Patton (2005) offered one especially useful method of simplifying text, which is to cover the page with transparency material, mark out the difficult words with a marker, and place the simplified text above. This allows the student to use the same textbook and read at a more appropriate level while also having a visual comparison of the higher reading level text.

Electronic versions of the text can support students who are unable to access even simplified written materials. Audio recordings of books and other classroom materials can provide students with access to information so that they can continue to learn vocabulary and concepts. Audio recorded books are available from commercial bookstores, from public libraries, and from nonprofit organizations such as Learning Ally and Bookshare; teachers or other support personnel can also create such materials. It is important to note that the use of audio recordings is not a substitute for learning to read, but rather a support activity to assist the student in continuing to learn the curricular content.

Study Guides

The use of a study guide can provide students with a support for engaging with content provided through a reading assignment. A study guide is a set of questions, fragments, or words that students complete or define while reading assigned content materials. The study guide provides an organizational structure that directs the student to the important facts. Bos and Vaughn (2015) suggested that effective study guides include

- specific information about the reading assignments (page numbers, title),
- learning objectives of the assignments,
- purpose statement for the assignment,
- introduction of key terms or vocabulary,
- activities for students to complete, and
- questions for students to answer as they read.

Learning Contracts

Learning contracts can be used to promote a sense of independence for all students. A *learning contract* is a written agreement made between the student and the teacher that includes the specified task, the requirements for successful completion, and any rules for conduct students must follow when working on their contracts. A learning contract can provide an opportunity to include student choice in the selection of sequence and tasks that the learner is to complete. Its specificity and concrete nature may make learning contracts especially useful for students with disabilities.

An in-depth knowledge of each student's readiness level, learning profile, and interests assists the teacher in designing the content of the learning tasks that will promote student growth. Tomlinson (2014, p. 139) outlined several elements teachers should consider including in the design of learning contracts, such as:

- Assume it is the teacher's responsibility to specify important content goals and make sure students work with them in a way that moves the student forward—and assume students can take on some of the responsibility for guiding their own learning.

- Delineate skills that need to be practiced and mastered.

- Ensure students will apply or use those skills in context (in other words, use the knowledge and skill to explore or extend an important understanding).

- Specify working conditions to which students must adhere during the contract time (e.g., student responsibilities, time constraints, homework and classwork involvement).

- Set positive consequences (e.g., continued opportunity to work independently) when students adhere to working conditions, and establish negative consequences (e.g., teacher makes work assignments and sets working parameters) if students do not adhere to working conditions.

- Establish criteria for successful completion and quality of work.

- Include both teacher and student signatures of agreement to the contract's terms.

Activity Stations and Learning Centers

Another modification that may be helpful for teachers in meeting the needs of all students in an inclusive classroom is the use of activity stations. Activity stations, set up in different locations throughout the classroom, provide opportunities for students to work on a selected learning activity that supports the lesson of the day. Activity stations provide activities that are directly related to the curriculum being studied and which teach, reinforce, or extend student knowledge, understanding, and skills. Activity stations may be based around *parallel activities*—activities that are focused on the lesson's content or goal but vary in difficulty or specific focus. Teachers can also use activity stations to respond to different learner needs through task selection and flexible grouping.

Activity stations are often considered to be the same as learning centers, but according to Tomlinson (2014), they are actually different. Activity stations supplement the content lesson being delivered that particular day, whereas learning centers are stand-alone areas that provide students with activities for developing proficiency in a certain concept or skill and are not specifically connected to a day's lesson. Activity stations are typically designed for use only for a short period of time—that is, for the length of the lesson they support.

Learning centers, on the other hand, are more often permanently placed in the classroom to enhance student interest and proficiency in a teacher-selected content area. As a result, teachers typically change and update the materials in the center on a regular basis and use a schedule to rotate all students through the site over the academic year. For example, an interest learning center is one that allows students to explore a particular interest and is not designed for mastery of knowledge or skills. Topics can be related to the unit of study but may address information outside the curriculum being studied. The choice of whether to use learning centers or activity stations is dependent on the teacher reviewing the content to be taught and students' readiness and proficiency.

Content modifications assist teachers in addressing individual learner needs while moving all students forward in learning the important content. Modification of the content also helps the teacher take the curricular standards required for a grade level or subject and transform them to fit the learner. This transformation can assist in reducing anxiety or boredom in the lives of children with exceptional needs. As Tomlinson et al. (2003) noted, "As a transformation in society and schools evolves, effective teachers in contemporary classrooms will have to learn to develop classroom routines that attend to, rather than ignore, learner variance in readiness, interest and learning profiles" (p. 121). This is particularly true as the inclusive classroom provides greater and more effective access to the general education curriculum for all students.

CHAPTER 5

How Does a Teacher Change the Learning Process?

The *learning process* is "how students go about making sense of ideas and information" (Tomlinson, 2001, p. 4). *Process*, therefore, is the selection of learning activities used to advance student acquisition of content selected by the teacher. Teachers consider how to match individual student learning profiles with learning strategies and teaching activities that will effectively support the learning process. It is the bridge that connects the learner to the curricular content. Simply stated, process is how teachers deliver content to students.

Research on the Learning Process

The No Child Left Behind Act of 2001 (formerly, Elementary and Secondary Education Act; as of fall 2015, Every Student Succeeds Act) and the Individuals With Disabilities Education Act both require that teachers select and use research-based strategies. In order to identify effective teaching strategies, research has focused on three main areas: learning modalities, multiple intelligences theory, and brain research. *Learning modalities* (also called *learning styles*) are the form in which learners prefer to receive information. Although the majority of learners are able to encode information in any of the three most often used learning modalities (i.e., visual, auditory, kinesthetic), they usually have a specific preference when offered the choice. *Visual learners* react to graphic organizers, maps, charts, and written words. *Auditory learners* respond to lectures, reading content aloud, songs, conversing, talking through a task, and group discussions. *Kinesthetic learners* are hands-on students and prefer tangible, concrete ways to explore new learning (Fogarty & Pete, 2011).

In 1983, Howard Gardner proposed a theory that each individual exhibits a personal profile of "intelligences" of different areas of strength, as opposed to the unitary view of intelligence being espoused at the time (Gardner, 1991, 1993). He identified and defined seven *multiple intelligences* (see Table 5.1). Teachers have found it useful to design process activities to engage students with the content through each student's stronger intelligence area. They also use the theory to help students produce a product that demonstrates their acquisition of the targeted content. By utilizing one to three of the multiple intelligences in the curriculum, the teacher delivers curricular content via multiple preferred accesses and offers students a variety of ways to demonstrate their competence with this content.

In the past decade, research on the human brain and how learning occurs has expanded. This research not only has broadened the scientific basis of differentiated instruction (Sousa & Tomlinson, 2011) but also actually provides a stronger theoretical base for differentiated instruction than either multiple intelligences or learning styles (Fogarty & Pete, 2011). Brain research findings support instruction

Table 5.1 Multiple Intelligences	
Area of strength	Explanation
Verbal/linguistic	Thinks in terms of words, uses words effectively, and has highly developed auditory skills. Learns through reading and playing word games or writing.
Visual/spatial	Thinks in terms of space and is aware of the environment. Learns through visual and physical images.
Intrapersonal/social	Builds understanding through interactions with others and learns best through group activities, seminars, and dialogues
Interpersonal/self	Understands his or her own interests and goals. Learns through independent study and introspection.
Mathematical/logical	Thinks abstractly, forms concepts, and sees relationships and patterns through the use of logic and reasoning. Learns best through the application of logic and solving questions.
Musical/rhythmic	Shows a sensitivity to music, rhythm, and sounds within the environment. Learns best by using music and rhythm as a background when studying and arranging content into lyrics and raps.
Bodily/kinesthetic	Effectively uses the body and has a well-developed awareness of the body. Learns best through hands-on and physical activities.

Note. See Gardner, 1999.

that is rich, stimulating, engaging, and focused on the learner—in Sousa and Tomlinson's words, revealing that "learning is as much a social process as it is a cognitive one" (2011, p. 14)—and, thus, revelations from brain research have informed classroom instructional practices (see Table 5.2).

Table 5.2 Brain Research Influence on Classroom Instruction	
Findings from research	Influence on classroom instruction
Each brain is uniquely organized. We all have personal preferences due to our unique experiences and interpretations of how our world works.	Incorporate student preference and interest in delivery of content, assignments, and products.
The brain's frontal lobe determines whether incoming information has meaning for the individual. If incoming information is perceived as an addition to a known pattern, then it is easier for students to learn and recall.	Link new information to content students have previously learned.
The frontal lobe (also called the executive center) also processes higher order thinking and problem solving. This is the place for new ideas and linking concepts.	Executive function skills (goal-directed, problem-solving behaviors) are essential to academic success. Provide clear expectations and directions as well as visual supports to enhance student development of these skills.
Emotions are processed in the brain. If it is flooded with emotional chemicals, retention of new materials is altered.	A negative learning environment tends to produce cortisol and shuts down learning for students. On the other hand, a positive learning environment tends to produce endorphins which makes it easier to process information.
Working memory can carry information without moving it to long-term memory if there is no reason to do so.	Working memory helps students make meaning of the information presented by connecting it to previous learning.
Learning requires focus and attention. Students learn what has meaning to them but can be diverted if distracted or diverted to a more interesting activity.	This kind of learning emphasizes understanding big ideas and is also engaging.

Instructional Strategies

Research in the areas of learning modalities, multiple intelligences, and brain-based learning has been translated into specific strategies that support differentiated instruction, such as direct instruction and cooperative learning. Teachers in inclusive classrooms use these strategies individually or collectively to effectively differentiate instruction and enhance learning for all students.

Direct Instruction

Direct instruction is routinely used in general education classrooms and is one of the most efficient methods of delivering instruction if the instruction employs a research-driven lesson design. In 1971, Hunter identified a lesson plan with seven elements (see Table 5.3) that has been widely used by teachers ever since. Although these elements are important, teachers can shift elements if the lesson would be improved by doing so. Direct instructional strategies that can be used in a differentiated classroom include metacognitive instruction, scaffolding and chunking, and whole-class, small-group, and individual instruction.

Table 5.3 Research-Based Lesson Plan Design	
Lesson plan component	Description
Anticipatory set	The hook
Learning objectives	Measurable while addressing both instructional standards and student needs
Input	Content, instructions, skills, tools
Modeling	Demonstration of skill or concept (e.g., "same or not same," "right or wrong")
Guided practice	Monitored student practice with feedback
Feedback	Immediate, specific, and relevant; given to the whole class or to individual students
Independent practice	Done by students on their own

Metacognitive instruction. Many students (with and without disabilities) need to be taught to learn how to organize academic tasks. Even if the teacher has employed all the recommendations given for a differentiated classroom, these students still will need tools to help them engage with the academic information presented. All three elements of differentiated instruction—content (what students are learning or how they access what they are learning), process (how they make sense of what they are learning), and product (how students show what they have learned)—are affected when students use metacognitive skills as they are thought to reorder the content within the student's brain for easier recall (Sousa & Tomlinson, 2011). The tools used in metacognitive instruction are readily recognized by teachers and include graphic organizers; mnemonics; imagery; story maps; and strategies such as RAFT, Tic-tac-toe, or Cubing (Tomlinson et al., 2003). Other places in the curriculum where metacognitive skills can be developed and practiced include remembering and applying information from course content, constructing sentences and paragraphs, editing written work, paraphrasing, and classifying information to be learned.

Scaffolding and chunking. *Scaffolding* is the step-by-step construction of a concept or skill that brings students along a logical pathway to support their acquisition of the targeted objective. Scaffolding is highly effective for learners with disabilities because of its use of "simplified language, teacher modeling, visuals and graphics, cooperative learning and hands-on experiences" (Ovando, Collier, & Combs, 2003, p. 345). When using this strategy, the teacher connects new knowledge to old knowledge so that the learner grows in the ability to employ the skill of scaffolding with future new content. This strategy is individualized because each learner is different. In scaffolding, the teacher's skill is one of dissecting the content into smaller parts to teach to the student. As the student learns the pieces, the teacher helps the student string the parts into a whole.

Chunking, on the other hand, refers to organizing or grouping separate pieces of information together to make them easier to learn. For example, when learning a phone number, a student might group the number in a meaningful pattern, such as three-digit area code, three digits, and then four digits. Thus, there is already a pattern established when the student needs to learn another new phone number. Indeed, the area code and the second group of three numbers may well be the same, so the new learning can easily be connected to the old via the pattern. Alternatively, a new pattern might be established where the area code (i.e., the first three numbers) may be the same, but the next group of three numbers and the final group of four numbers are different.

Whole-class instruction. Whole-class instruction is one of the most familiar formats used by teachers, but it can be improved by using differentiated instruction. Whole-class instruction can include activities that address multiple intelligences or learning styles and preferences (Bender, 2012). For example, teachers can design a whole-class lesson using a minimum of three modalities: lecture (auditory), illustration or video (visual), and manipulatives or model-building (hands-on or kinesthetic). Teachers also can ask varied questions to address different readiness levels of the students.

Small-group instruction. Teachers frequently use small-group instruction to assist students in remedying an academic or skill deficiency. To do this, a small group is formed and given intense, explicit instruction. It is then disbanded when the learners have accomplished the learning objective. This flexible grouping allows teachers to form and re-form groups as needed. For example, a small group can follow whole-class instruction to check for understanding when new material or skills are presented. Flexible grouping can be based on a variety of student traits or needs including achievement data, interests, preferred approaches to learning, similar or dissimilar traits, and individual needs (making sure that students come to see themselves as working in a variety of groupings throughout a unit of study).

Individual instruction. Students often learn more quickly when the teacher has the opportunity to work with them on a one-on-one basis. One advantage with this type of instruction is that the teacher can prompt or correct at the moment when an error occurs. A second advantage is that the teacher can gain insight into the student's learning issue(s) and thus can tailor future lessons to better support the student's learning.

Cooperative Learning

Cooperative learning is a well-researched, powerful strategy that has been shown effective with diverse learners (Hoover, 2009; Hourcade & Bauwens, 2003). Thus, cooperative learning methods are often used to differentiate process activities within a general education classroom. Fogarty and Pete (2011, p. 86) used the acronym BUILD to differentiate cooperative learning from small-group instruction:

- B = Build in higher order thinking (predict, analyze, conclude).
- U = Unite the team (specify team roles and responsibilities, team tasks, and team rewards).
- I = Include individual accountability (require personal responsibility for the information).
- L = Look back and reflect (learn about collaborative work).
- D = Develop social skills (focus on communication, leadership, and team-work).

There are many cooperative learning strategies for use in classroom collaboration. Most are well-known with directions readily available (e.g., jigsaw, numbered heads together, think-pair-share, student team learning, team assisted individualization, student teams-achievement divisions, team-games-tournament, cooperative integrated reading and composition). What is most important to remember is that cooperative learning methods are excellent for differentiating instruction for all types of learners.

Selecting and Designing Process Strategies

Teachers often find it helpful to have a basic, general guide to assist them in selecting and designing process strategies appropriate for use in their inclusive classrooms. Tomlinson's *How to Differentiate Instruction in Mixed-Ability Classrooms* (1995) was the first such guide to assist teachers in designing strategies likely to assure the success of all students in inclusive settings, including students with disabilities, and continues to provide teachers with a map for their selection and use of process strategies in their classrooms. The basic components of selecting and designing process strategies include:

- Have a clear purpose.
- Focus on a few key ideas.
- Guide students in understanding the ideas and the relationships among them.
- Offer opportunities to explore ideas through varied modes (e.g., visual, kinesthetic, spatial, musical).
- Help students relate new information to previous understanding.
- Match students' level of readiness.

Process is the bridge that connects the learner to the curricular content within the learning environment. The process for how students come to learn important content in school requires teachers to utilize a variety of sound, effective strategies in the inclusive differentiated classroom. Expanding research focused on the areas of multiple intelligences, learning modalities, and the brain supports many of the strategies used by teachers in differentiating instruction. As teachers continue to use differentiated instruction to meet the needs of *all* their students, this research base will continue to grow—as will the strategies teachers use to support the learners they serve.

CHAPTER 6

How Does a Teacher Modify the Product?

Student progress reporting and monitoring are essential facets of teacher responsibility for all students and perhaps especially for students with disabilities. For students with disabilities, their individualized education programs (IEPs) include progress information on benchmarks or short-term objectives leading to successful completion of the IEP annual goals. In order for the teacher to assess whether student learning has occurred, some form of product or observable outcome of that learning must follow. Tomlinson (1999) defined *products* as "vehicles through which students demonstrate and extend what they have learned" (p. 11). In other words, the product is the planned culmination or result of the learning activity, lesson, or interaction that the teacher presents. The product represents a tangible assessment showing that the student has acquired the knowledge, understanding, and skills that were the focus of the lesson.

The issue for teachers is that the typical product format or the assessment system used in general education classrooms may not be effective in accurately assessing the knowledge level of students with diverse learning needs, including those with disabilities and others considered at risk. Just as some students may require modifications in the learning environment, content, and process, they and others may also need modifications in the ways they are able to demonstrate their success in learning the content.

Types of Products

When designing a lesson with its subsequent assessment of whether the student has learned the skills or is proficient in the content being studied, two forms of products can be considered: concrete products and abstract products (see Renzulli, Leppien, & Hays's 2000 Multiple Menu Model). *Concrete products* are physical constructions (e.g., written essays, videos, dramatizations, experiments) created by students for the evaluation of the learning and interaction with the content and process that have occurred in the classroom. Renzulli et al. (2000) grouped concrete products into seven categories (see Table 6.1): artistic products, performance products, spoken products, visual products, models/construction products, leadership products, and written products. Deciding which of these products might most effectively illustrate successful student learning is often dependent on the goals of the lesson and the learning preferences of individual students.

Table 6.1 Concrete Products	
Type of product	Description/examples
Artistic	Artistic products demonstrate student learning through creative and graphic development of a physical product (e.g., murals, storyboards, comic strips, drawings, photographs, mobiles, diorama, collage, paints, pottery, maps).
Performance	Performance products evaluate student knowledge through product development and performance of skits, role-playing, mime, puppet shows, musical performance, reenactments, and interpretive song.
Spoken	Spoken products allow students to present learned information in an oral format such as speeches, poetry readings, songs, announcements, newscasts, oral reports, sign language, and rap songs.
Visual	Visual products may overlap with other types of products, and include videos, book jackets, posters, storyboards, comic strips, software demonstrations, digital or electronic designs, diagrams, set design, and photography.
Model/construction	Model and construction products incorporate building or construction of models such as relief maps, terrariums, diorama, ant farms, birdhouses, bulletin boards, three-dimensional figures, robots, machines, and furniture.
Leadership	Leadership products are designed to showcase student learning and demonstration of leadership skills. These activities include giving a speech, role playing, participating in a debate, organizing a business or a fundraising event, editing a newspaper, and hosting a chat room or discussion group on the Internet.
Written	Written products include brochures, captions, charts, interview questions, recipes, newspaper articles, web pages, lists, timelines, story problems, and graphic organizers.

Note. See Renzulli, Leppien, & Hays, 2000.

Sometimes evaluation through a concrete product presentation is not feasible. In these cases, evaluation of knowledge may need to occur through abstract products. *Abstract products* are specific student behaviors identified by the teacher as indicators to verify that student learning has occurred. Abstract products are generally divided into two categories: cognitive structures and affective structures (see Renzulli et al., 2000, pp. 68–69). For both categories, teacher observation of student behaviors and data collection reveals whether a student has mastered a concept or skill. Cognitive-structure behaviors include the use of metacognition, perseverance in completing a project, and using problem-solving strategies. Affective-structure behaviors include student empathy for others, self-concept, and appreciation—and may also include data on behavioral and social skills that are more and more essential to many students' IEPs.

Types of Assessment

In order to most effectively meet the needs of students with exceptional needs in the inclusive classroom, teachers should use assessment procedures that are more comprehensive and powerful than traditional paper-and-pencil tests in evaluating student learning. Common, traditional assessment options (e.g., commercial tests, curriculum tests, criterion-referenced skill inventories and checklists, teacher-made instruction) tend to be norm-referenced and thus may not be particularly instructionally useful for students with disabilities. Alternatives to these assessment procedures include authentic assessment, portfolio assessment, presentations (for example through the use of oral accounts or through a combination of using technology to show what a student has learned), and scoring guides or rubrics—all of which hold considerable promise for generating richer and more educationally useful information for teachers.

Authentic Assessment

Authentic assessment includes measures based in the "real world" in order to allow students to demonstrate their knowledge and skills. It differs from traditional assessments in that the student is directly assessed on the activity (e.g., a demonstration, project, or presentation) in a real-life situation. When using authentic assessment, the teacher designs and uses meaningful, complex, and relevant learning activities to decide if the student has learned the knowledge, understanding, or skill that was being taught. Authentic assessments would require students to apply what they have learned to a context that is familiar to their lives or is viewed as one that professionals in that field use. It does not require that students complete the task outside of school since it is likely that teachers would need to guide students in managing such projects in order for them to meet success.

Teachers may need to provide timelines and break-up larger projects into smaller parts so that a larger authentic assessment does not overwhelm students who may struggle with organization or are easily frustrated with multi-step directions.

Portfolio Assessment

Portfolios can be an especially useful form of authentic assessment. According to Imhof and Picard (2009), a *portfolio* is "a focused collection of diverse documents and artifacts that ... reflect a person's learning process" (p. 149). Because portfolios are easily tailored to meet specific student needs, they are extremely versatile to use as a concrete product in a differentiated classroom (Mastropieri & Scruggs, 2014).

Portfolios are typically constructed as teachers and students work together collecting and reflecting on student products over a specified period of time. The type and number of products to be included in the portfolio should also be decided through an interactive dialogue between the student and the teacher. Examples of portfolio products include book logs, student self-evaluations, math projects, results from examinations, video recordings or photographs of science experiments, individually developed semantic maps or graphic organizers, and research reports.

Salend (2011) identified six steps for teachers to use if they plan to assess student learning through a portfolio product:

1. Identify the goals of the portfolio.
2. Determine the type of portfolio.
3. Select a variety of real-classroom products that address the goals of the portfolio.
4. Establish procedures for collecting, storing, organizing, and noting the significance of students' portfolios.
5. Record the significance of items included in students' portfolios and help students reflect on them.
6. Review and evaluate portfolios, and share them with others. (pp. 484–488)

In addition, teachers who are considering using portfolios as a form of evaluating their students' proficiency on a selected content lesson might incorporate Batzle's (1992) basic principles of portfolio assessment and evaluation:

- Portfolio assessment and evaluation is ongoing and gathered over time.
- Portfolio assessment and evaluation embraces different developmental levels.
- Portfolio assessment and evaluation matches and guides instruction.
- Portfolio assessment and evaluation is unique to each child.
- Portfolio assessment and evaluation emphasizes what kids know.

- Portfolio assessment and evaluation involves teachers and children conferencing and evaluating together.

- Portfolio assessment and evaluation provides a variety of evidence through process and product samples. (pp. 13–19)

Scoring Guides or Rubrics

Scoring guides or rubrics are grading guidelines that teachers can use when evaluating students for proficiency in and learning of the content of the specific lessons (Jackson & Larkin, 2002). Rubrics can be either individually or interactively developed; individually developed rubrics are usually prepared by the teacher, whereas an interactively developed rubric is jointly developed by the teacher and student, by a group of students, or by peer pairs. More specifically, rubrics are used with specified criteria to indicate the level of proficiency of the student and provide both the student and the teacher with a clear guide for an acceptable product. The major reason for using a scoring guide or rubric when evaluating students, especially those with disabilities, is that the grading of modified products can be made more objective and consistent.

When a teacher decides to use a rubric as a method for assessing the understanding of content or the skill proficiency that a student has accomplished, there are two steps in the rubric development process. The first step is to decide on the facets or components of the rubric (i.e., what content knowledge is to be evaluated). The second component, a decision on the rating scale size and criteria, is more difficult because there are no specific rules for deciding how to evaluate the content, process, and product of the assessment. The criteria and the evaluation guidelines are dependent on the teacher's knowledge of the goals of the learning activity as well as the level of the students in the classroom. Generally, grading scales on rubrics are structured with three levels: below expectations, meets expectations, and exceeds expectations. The teacher develops a clear, concise set of criteria for each level and presents the rubric to students to ensure that they understand the criteria and its use in evaluating their products. Concrete examples are especially helpful as guides for students with developmental disabilities, who may need assistance understanding the criteria and their use, to understand the process and how the rubric will be used.

Many teachers who incorporate differentiated instructional methods into their classes are concerned with the evaluation of students with exceptional needs. The issue of fair evaluation practices that do not lessen the quality of the curriculum for all students continues to be of concern. Both concrete products and abstract products can provide valuable evaluative information. Authentic assessment, especially portfolio assessment, can be useful in determining educational progress and success in students with developmental disabilities. Incorporating scoring rubrics when using authentic and portfolio assessment can further enhance the validity and reliability of the evaluation procedures and the resulting product.

CHAPTER 7

What Does Differentiated Instruction in an Inclusive Classroom Look Like?

Today, most teachers have heard of differentiated instruction—although many fear that it will take too much time, or they are simply overwhelmed and do not know where to start. Foster (2015) suggested that a teacher can make one simple change to the daily lesson plan by targeting two students who have not yet benefited from the daily instruction. This can be accomplished by identifying the students' differences and interests and, then, planning differentiated instruction based on concepts presented in this book. Foster felt that if this were done weekly, the teacher would evolve and employ a differentiated approach to all instruction. If followed for a year, imagine the repertoire of instructional modifications that teachers could create in their classrooms (Foster, 2015)!

To help put it all together, we provide examples of two inclusive general education classrooms whose teachers implemented differentiated instruction practices. Perhaps their journeys will offer answers to typical questions that arise when considering how to use the differentiated instruction approach to teaching.

Educator: Amanda, Second-Grade Teacher

Amanda is an elementary school classroom teacher who has been teaching for 3 years. Presently, she is working on her Master's degree in Curriculum and Instruction with an emphasis in the area of gifted and talented education. She has a classroom of 25 second-graders in a school located in a "bedroom" community near a large Midwestern city. The school district recently adopted a philosophy of inclusion, with the general education classroom as the primary placement for all students with exceptional needs.

Amanda's class includes 11 boys and 14 girls ranging in age from 6 to 9 years old. Of these 25 students, there are five for whom English is not the primary language, two who have been officially identified as gifted and talented, four who receive special education services, and one who has a Section 504 accommodation plan. Of the four students with individualized education programs (IEPs), three students (Mark, Cindy, and Brian) are diagnosed with a specific learning disability, and one student (Diana) has moderate intellectual disability and cerebral palsy. The one student (John) on a Section 504 accommodation plan has been diagnosed with attention deficit hyperactivity disorder.

Learning Environment Considerations

As Amanda reviews her "planning pyramid" (Schumm, Vaughn, & Leavell, 1994; see Chapter 2) and the areas to be considered when differentiating instruction for her diverse classroom, she decides to focus first on her classroom environment. The issues that must be addressed are physical accessibility (both within the classroom and the school), the social structure of the classroom (including instructional grouping), and the classroom climate. What should Amanda concentrate on first? She decides to first examine the current physical arrangement of her room using the Learning Environment Checklist (see Figure 3.1).

Amanda notes that the student desks in her classroom are in rows except for two tables on the side of the class near her own desk. These two tables are the desks for Diana and John. For most of the day, Diana and John sit at one or both of these tables, where they receive help from a paraprofessional. John is also assisted during the morning by a behavioral therapist. Diana leaves the classroom for occupational therapy, and a speech therapist comes in periodically to help Diana with her picture communication board. For the most part, John sits at the table away from the other students because he is easily distracted and needs redirection by the teacher assistant. He also displays some defiant behaviors.

For most of Amanda's lessons, she uses whole-group direct instruction followed by independent seatwork and sometimes paired-group work. Amanda quickly realizes that her class arrangement facilitates independence but not social or leadership interactions or any flexible seating arrangements or grouping. In fact, she notes that two of her students, Diana and John, are not even part of her "whole group" and therefore have limited, if any, peer interactions during the school day.

Group seating arrangement. The first thing Amanda decides is to arrange the students' desks in groups of five, using mixed-ability grouping. She has studied the learners in her classroom, so she knows her students well. Amanda is confident that she can appropriately select students for each group. She plans to group students using different student characteristics such as common interests; varying social and leadership skills; and varying abilities, background knowledge, and experiences. Amanda also decides that she will try to keep this seating arrangement for at least 3 months. She would like each group of students to get to know one another well and to have a stable "home" group to return to when she uses other types of flexible grouping for classroom instruction.

Amanda also knows that she will place Diana next to and across from her peers, and she will place John on the end of the five-desk grouping so that his desk will be in a location that will allow him some movement when needed. If he needs to move his desk slightly away or turn it completely around from the group, he will be easily able to do so. Amanda will try a desk divider to use when John is too distracted by an activity or the other students in his group. Also, John's old desk (the table by the side wall) will now be used as a learning center because it will be right behind him and he will be able to turn his chair around and use the table when needed.

Up until this time, Amanda has grouped her students only for reading instruction. She has a reading corner, so she placed students together for reading based on their reading levels. She now believes she needs to more closely monitor her reading readiness groups to ensure student movement among the groups. Although Amanda continually monitors their progress, she feels she may not be moving students from their established reading readiness groups as often as she should. Upon further reflection, she thinks she might be able to enhance student learning by establishing some periods of reading instruction based on student interest instead of only by reading level or other levels of academic achievement.

Amanda's review of her mathematics instruction leads her to determine that she can meet the learning needs of her students in math using differentiated instruction. She concludes that introducing flexible grouping and providing math instruction through learning centers would be more beneficial for her students than always using whole-class instruction.

Flexible grouping using cooperative learning. After reviewing her physical arrangements, Amanda realizes that her focus on differentiated instruction in mathematics begins with the use of flexible grouping arrangements. She would like to start implementing cooperative learning strategies because of her interest in developing social and leadership skills within her class. Amanda decides to begin with teaching the students cooperative social skills, including learning how to give positive feedback to each other, take turns, and listen to and encourage or cue peer responses. She will initiate one social skill at a time. During group instruction, Amanda plans to implement student activities that will focus on learning a particular social or leadership skill.

Because Amanda has had little experience with cooperative learning, she will assign students to a group of five, with a total of five cooperative learning math groups. She has made a rotation schedule for the five math groups. After Amanda implements 10 minutes of review and practice with the whole group, each group will spend 10 minutes rotating through each math center. Amanda will be at one designated math center where she will guide students by using mini-lessons, through guided practice, and by working with students individually. Because she has three tables for her math centers, students will rotate through these centers. Amanda will also develop two "centers" for students to use at their desks. At least once a week, she will have her guided math center set up for students to play a math game independently. This will give Amanda the opportunity to rotate through the four other centers and monitor student progress. When Amanda and her students become comfortable with working in guided math centers of five, she then will introduce other flexible group arrangements for some periods of their math instruction.

Content Modifications

In mathematics, Amanda has been working on the Common Core mathematics standards for second grade, including "Tell and write time from analog and digital clocks to the nearest 5 minutes, using a.m. and p.m." To this point, her lessons have addressed goals and objectives related to the review of telling time to the quarter hour and solving time-related problems. Even though the majority of her students have been part of these whole-group lessons, some students have not been successful.

Amanda decides to change her instructional method from whole-class instruction and individual seatwork activities to differentiated instructional activities based initially on individual student readiness levels. Amanda will assess her students with a curriculum-based, criterion-referenced inventory to determine what time-related skills each student has mastered and which skills each student needs to develop.

Because Diana requires additional background experiences and skills to learn how to tell time, Amanda will implement an alternative curriculum for Diana using curriculum overlapping. Diana has a number of objectives from her IEP that can be incorporated in the time-related mathematics lessons. For example, because she is learning to match numbers from 1 to 5, Diana will work on matching numbers from 1 to 5 on an analog clock. Other areas of skill development that will be addressed for Diana will include taking turns, using a turning motion to change the hand positions on the classroom clock, and initiating requests using her picture communication board.

Brian, on the other hand, is learning to count by fives and recognize numbers from 1 to 60. He will continue with learning to tell time to the quarter hour. High-readiness students, including Cindy, will work on telling time at 5-minute intervals and solving word problems related to the addition of time intervals. One of her peers will help Cindy read the word problems. Amanda expects that after all students are assessed, a few other students may need the content modified to meet their individual needs. As instruction progresses, she will pre-assess students before she introduces a new topic in the math unit. This will allow her to change students either from groups or to different readiness levels within the math learning centers.

Process Modifications

After assessing her students, Amanda decides to use her guided math center and rotate through the other centers (on some days) to provide direct instruction to individuals or the group as needed. She will also use universal design for learning strategies (see National Center on Universal Design for Learning, http://www.udlcenter.org/) and multilevel instruction techniques such as scaffolding with simplified language and examples for students to model. Amanda's math centers that are focused on time will include a variety of materials to provide students with multiple means of engagement (e.g., Judy clocks, iPad apps, and the classroom clock) and tasks such as games and flash cards at different levels of readiness. Activities will be color-coded and numbered to reflect the knowledge and experience required for completing each activity. Also, Amanda will set up learning center contracts with each student. In structuring these contracts, she will choose some activities that each student will complete and will allow students to choose some activities for themselves. A timeline will be developed for students to keep track of their individual activities and schedules for completion.

Also, Amanda will plan a number of multilevel instructional activities to be incorporated in her group activities. For example, in Diana's group, each student will have his or her own color cards. These cards will be shuffled. As each student's color card comes up on the pile, that student will perform the time-related task requested on the card. Using cooperative learning, one student will be the checker, one student will be the facilitator, and another student will be the encourager. Students and their roles will change periodically so that they develop many cooperative learning social and leadership skills while in second grade. Diana's time-related cards will be read by another student in her group.

Some of Diana's tasks are based on her IEP objectives. For example, Diana will be requested to turn the hands of the clock. When she stops, another student in the group must tell the time to the hour. On some turns, Diana will be requested to point to the correct number (1, 2, or 3) on the classroom clock when the associated number appears on her card. In addition, before taking her turn, Diana will initiate or be requested to point to the picture of the math card on her communication board, thus indicating that it is her turn.

Brian will also need similar accommodations to his tasks cards and activities during these group lessons and practice sessions. His tasks will reflect his entry point in the instruction. Some students within the group will have entry points that require higher level thinking skills. Their tasks in the groups will be more advanced because they will be expected to perform such tasks as indicating what time it will be in 5 minutes, giving the correct time using pictures of analog clocks, solving word problems using time terminology, and simple addition and subtraction of time intervals.

Product Modifications

Amanda will bring students together to introduce a new topic at their math readiness level. Students at each level will complete a pre-assessment prior to the introduction of new topics, which will help Amanda to determine if she needs to move students to different readiness levels at the math centers so that they focus on activities that meet their needs and also show their progress.

Amanda plans to use three types of assessment to check students' understanding of the concept of time. First, when students are working together in their math center groups, she will develop checklists for the checker in each group to record data (see Figure 7.1). Each student's checklist will reflect the tasks that the individual performs in the group and at the math learning center. On some days, Amanda will move from center to center to give individual and group instruction, listen to students' verbal responses, and monitor their performance as indicated on their checklists. She will also use a checklist to monitor student progress at her guided math center.

Second, Amanda will request that each student select one completed product that has been assigned to them at any one of the math centers. The product will be one that demonstrates successful learning of the concept they have studied during the unit on "Telling Time." The products chosen may vary from student to student and may include such products as drawings, demonstrations, oral responses or reports, created practice worksheets with answer keys, and results from a time-related game.

Third, Amanda will use authentic assessment. She will check each student on time-related problems in real-life situations at school throughout the unit on time to assess understanding and application of the time concepts that students are learning. She will use varying levels of questions to elicit responses. Diana will use her picture communication board to provide her answers.

Co-Teachers: Luis and Kayla, High School Biology

Luis is a high school biology teacher. He recently received his Master of Science in Biology. Although he has taught science for 5 years at a middle school in an urban school district, this is his first year teaching at one of the district's high schools. The superintendent asked Luis to take this position because he had successfully included students with disabilities in his eighth-grade Life Science class. He will teach one section of Biology 1 and three sections of Biology 2. This year, the administrators in his school district decided to expand inclusive education at the high school level and felt Luis could provide differentiated instruction for his Biology 1 students. It is also hoped that he and Kayla, a special education teacher who has been assigned to co-teach with him, will support other faculty in this new undertaking.

Figure 7.1 Amanda's Math Center Checklist			
Student's Name and ID#	Date/ Task # Completed	Completed Correctly Yes　　No	Comments
1.			
2.			
3.			
4.			
5.			
6.			
7.			
8.			
9.			
10.			
11.			
12.			
13.			
14.			
15.			
16.			
17.			
18.			
19.			
20.			

Kayla has been teaching for 3 years and has provided resource support to students with disabilities. Kayla has also co-taught in two high school math classes, but this is the first time she will be co-teaching in a biology class. Luis and Kayla's Biology 1 class has 24 ninth-grade students: 14 boys and 10 girls, ranging in age from 14 to 16 years old. There are five students for whom English is not their primary language, three who have been identified as gifted and talented, and five who receive special education services. Of those five students receiving special education services, two students have been identified as having intellectual disability (Danny and Janis); two students (Maria and Jamie) have been identified as having a specific learning disability; and one student (Mark) who has been identified as having an emotional or behavioral disability.

Co-Teaching and Collaboration

Because Luis and Kayla both have been trained and have taught as co-teachers before, they know that they will need to discuss important classroom issues prior to beginning the unit with their students. They are fully aware that they are equal partners and will plan, instruct, and assess the students in their shared classroom. Most important is that they both recognize that ongoing communication is a must. Thus, as Luis and Kayla review their "planning pyramid" and the areas to be considered when employing differentiated instruction in a mixed-ability classroom, they decide their first focus will be on the content to be addressed. The next issues they must address are the safety issues involved in teaching science, the methodological and philosophical differences involved in teaching through an experiential or constructivist approach, the use of manipulatives to enhance learning, and the issue of concrete versus critical thinking as the focus of instruction.

Although this is the first time that Luis has had a student with a moderate intellectual disability in his class, he has had students with various mild disabilities in his science classes in the past. He has made a number of modifications to the curriculum over the years, but he often feels overwhelmed when trying to teach the academic content to all students. This year, Luis and Kayla's goals are to focus on reasonable objectives for each student and to include Danny in as many science activities as possible. Luis and Kayla decide that each time they plan a lesson, they need to keep in mind the three questions of the planning pyramid:

- What will *all* students learn?
- What will *most* (but not all) students learn?
- What will *some* students learn?

The first unit Luis and Kayla will be teaching relates to cells. The concept on which they will focus is, "All living things are made of cells that perform functions necessary for life." However, within this unit on cells, Luis and Kayla will embed scientific inquiry, technology, and mathematics. Throughout the unit, students will be experimenting, collecting, recording, and analyzing data while seeking answers to questions developed for further investigation.

Luis and Kayla decide that at the end of the first part of the unit, all students will be able to describe the three parts of the cell theory and to label the two types of cells (prokaryotic and eukaryotic cells). Most students will be able to describe the structure and function of each component of these types of cells. They will be able to describe the structure and function of the four main types of organic macromolecules found in living things (proteins, carbohydrates, lipids, and nucleic acids). They will be able to compare and contrast animal and plant cells. Some students will be able to distinguish between an organism and a community of cells.

Learning Environment Considerations

Luis and Kayla must address the environment in the classroom and how it needs to be modified in order to assure successful learning for all students. They determine that two of the highest environmental considerations are how to group students and classroom organization.

Instructional grouping. Because this is the beginning unit on cells, many students in Luis and Kayla's class have not used a microscope or handled glass slides. Introductory lessons and practice sessions using the microscope and related materials will be part of this unit. Luis and Kayla decide that for these lessons and practice sessions, they will pair students and set up learning stations based on microscope use and safety procedures. They will carefully select student pairs based on a buddy system, with one student who is more familiar with these procedures paired with another student who is less familiar. They will continue to use pairs and double pairs throughout this unit, occasionally changing pairs as their assessment of students' knowledge and their application of the concepts indicate. Whenever possible, Luis and Kayla will also change pairs for lessons where students share an interest in the content or format of a product (e.g., writing an experiment report, giving an oral presentation, creating a poster or graphic organizer). Kayla has suggested that perhaps they could set up a peer-mentor program with the Advanced Placement Biology class at the high school. They decide to investigate this possibility with their principal.

Classroom organization. Luis and Kayla also realize that they and their classroom need to be organized. They understand that they will need to organize the student groups carefully and that they will need to develop good signals for students to recognize that they will be changing centers. The lab itself will be organized so that students know where to find materials. These materials will be clearly labeled and accessible before class begins. Luis and Kayla will work together to determine how they will establish the organization of materials and routines. They will have students practice these routines before beginning an experiment or working in their center.

Luis and Kayla use a list of questions to guide them in planning their co-teaching classroom arrangements; they intend to revisit this list periodically to ensure that student needs and preferences are still being met:

- Will students work alone or in groups?
- If alone, will students choose the task or will the teachers?
- If in groups, will students choose the task or will the teachers?
- If in groups, what size group would be best?

- If in groups, will it be heterogeneous or homogeneous in terms of interest or goal?

- If in groups, will teachers assign students to groups or will students be allowed to choose?

Content Modifications

To begin the unit on cells, Luis and Kayla decide that they will have students work together using a worksheet for microscope safety. This worksheet, outlines the procedures for using a microscope safely step by step; Kayla mentions that in order for the worksheet's procedures to be more accessible to Danny and Maria, it should include photos. Because Maria responds well to using the computer, Luis decides to have students from one of the high school technology classes come in before the unit starts and take pictures of a student demonstration of the microscope procedures using a digital video camera. These step-by-step video shorts with accompanying verbal directions will be placed on the computer at one of the learning stations. All students will have access to the videos for review, but Maria will be encouraged to use the computer as needed whenever the use of the microscope is required. Also available to the entire class are the still photographs displayed as a classroom chart to use as a reference as they complete their worksheet assignment. Both items will remain available if students need them during the unit on cells.

In beginning the unit, Luis and Kayla will give the students a brief curriculum-based pre-assessment on cells addressing the objectives they have identified based on the planning pyramid questions. The pair will also use their knowledge of relevant student characteristics (i.e., student interests, preferences for learning materials, readiness) to modify the content for individuals or small groups of students as necessary.

For this unit, Luis and Kayla plan to provide students with a number of ways to learn and process the content and to demonstrate their understanding. Luis and Kayla will share in modifying the content for a number of students by

- altering the text (primarily by omitting extraneous details and reducing the reading level of the text);

- highlighting important information and critical features;

- providing study guides, practice sheets, and graphic organizers;

- providing multiple examples to explain concepts;

- having students use web-based visual dictionaries; and

- allowing students to use a self-study program with practice exercises on the computer.

Luis had developed some supplemental materials in previous years, and this year Kayla will help him modify additional materials specifically for Danny and Maria. Kayla will preview the material with Maria and Danny the day before a new concept will be presented, too, which will allow Maria and Danny to be familiar with the new material before it is taught to the whole group.

Although Danny will mainly be provided with an alternative curriculum, he will functionally participate with the other students. Danny is interested in science materials and has had experience observing through a telescope and a microscope. (Danny's older brother, who is now in college majoring in chemistry, was in Luis's class 6 years ago. Danny's brother and parents help to reinforce activities done in school.) Luis and Kayla will work primarily on objectives from Danny's IEP, including such skills as taking turns, learning the name of his partner and group members as depicted on his picture communication board, and initiating requests for assistance using the sign for help. Luis and Kayla believe that using the microscope and other learning centers and activity stations in the classroom will provide opportunities for Danny to work on these IEP objectives. Danny will not be required to master the cell unit objectives identified for all students; Luis and Kayla have identified several modified objectives for Danny, such as using a microscope safely, distinguishing a plant cell from an animal cell based on color, and placing a label on the nucleus in plant and animal cells depicted in various formats.

The content for Maria and some of the other students will be modified by simplifying the text and using study guides and graphic organizers that will be in written text as well as in a computer text file. The study guide on the computer will be linked to drill and practice exercises. The computer will be located in one of the learning centers set up in the room and made available to all students.

Process Modifications

Although Luis and Kayla have decided to use pairs for most activities, for some activities they will give students a choice to work alone or will implement jigsaw groups or other cooperative learning strategies. For the jigsaw groups, pairs of students will work together (making six groups of two pairs each; $n = 4$ students per group) to learn new vocabulary words and to expand on topics of student interests. For each group, Luis and Kayla will ensure that students vary in abilities so that all groups will have one student who can explain, demonstrate, and help others with the content or problems.

Luis and Kayla also plan to provide whole-group instruction for short periods of time (i.e., mini-lectures) during each class period. This direct instruction will include demonstrations or review of content at some of the learning centers set up throughout the classroom. They plan to use various types of co-teaching models for this instruction (e.g., team teaching, parallel teaching, and alternate teaching, see Table 7.1 and Marilyn Friend, Inc., 2007). For the rest of the science period, pairs of students will work at the learning stations. Each individual in the pair will have some tasks that are the same as his or her partner's, and some that are different.

Table 7.1 Co-Teaching Models and Actions	
Model	Actions
One teach, one observe	One teacher instructs students while the other observes students to monitor learning and understanding of material. This teacher collects student data to ensure everyone understands the lesson.
Station teaching	Teachers create stations in order to instruct students in small groups. Students rotate stations, receiving instruction from both teachers.
Parallel teaching	In order to differentiate instruction, teachers divide the class into groups and teach different groups within the class similar material.
Alternative teaching	One teacher instructs a large group of students, and the other teacher works with smaller groups of students
Teaming	Both teachers instruct the class together, alternating presentation of material
One teach, one assist	One teacher instructs students, while the other teacher provides students individualized instruction and assistance
If one of you is doing this…	The other can be doing this…
Lecturing	Modeling note taking on board/overhead and ensuring "brain breaks" to help students process lecture information
Giving instructions orally	Modeling writing down instructions and repeating or clarifying any difficult concept
Checking for understanding with large heterogeneous group of students	Checking for understanding with small heterogeneous group of students

Table 7.1 Co-Teaching Models and Actions (cont'd)	
If one of you is doing this…	The other can be doing this…
Circulating and providing one-on-one support	Providing direct instruction to whole class
Prepping half of the class for one side of a debate	Prepping the other half of the class for the opposing side of the debate
Facilitating a silent activity	Circulating and checking for comprehension
Providing whole-class instruction	Circulating and using proximity for behavior management
Re-teaching or pre-teaching with a small group	Monitoring large group as they work on practice materials
Facilitating sustained silent reading	Reading aloud quietly with a small group and previewing upcoming information
Reading a test aloud to a group of students	Proctoring a test silently with a group of students
Creating basic lesson plans for standards, objectives, and content curriculum	Providing suggestions for modifications, accommodations, and activities for diverse learners
Facilitating stations or groups	Facilitating stations or groups
Explaining a new concept	Conducting role-play or modeling a concept and asking clarifying questions
Considering modification needs	Considering enrichment opportunities

Note. Reprinted from *The Survival Guide for New Special Education Teachers*, by C. Martin and C. Hauth, 2015, p. 32. Copyright 2015 Council for Exceptional Children.

To engage students, Luis and Kayla will allow for choices depending on the tasks at that center. The learning centers will provide students with the opportunity to learn and demonstrate understanding using a variety of modes and at varying levels (see Table 7.2). Luis and Kayla have set up activities that are tiered at two levels (or more) so all students can participate at their own entry level. Based on these two levels, Kayla and Luis will develop further changes of the content or process for those students requiring any additional modifications or adaptations.

Luis and Kayla also have set up a "conference center" they will use to meet with individual students. Students will rotate through centers, based on a weekly schedule. Some students may need to spend more time at some centers than others;

Table 7.2 Luis and Kayla's Learning Centers	
Learning Centers	Activities
Learning Center 1 (Located in Biology classroom)	Has materials for students to construct three dimensional models of different types of cells. Materials might include, but are not limited to, Styrofoam sheets, clay or Play-Doh, ribbons or wires, poster board, glue, and markers.
Learning Center 2 (Located in Biology classroom)	Has computers for viewing information about cells, with varying types of questions to challenge students at their readiness level. Students can work individually or with a partner at the computers.
Learning Center 3 (Located in Biology classroom)	Has materials to create various types of cells that need to be labeled according to type, compared identifying similarities, and contrasted identifying differences. Work sheets are provided to all students providing a Venn diagrams for students to complete writing the type of cell as a title and the Venn diagram showing the overlapping similarities and the disparate sections as difference.
Learning Centers 4-7 (Located in Biology classroom)	Students work independently, in pairs, or as a group. All have microscopes with prepared slides for viewing cells, accompanied by different types of worksheets and data recording sheets. Centers also have slides and materials to make and label new slides for viewing. Also available are practice worksheets, activities, and games to check knowledge and understanding according to student's individual learning objectives. Materials are available for a wide range of student abilities and interests.

Table 7.2 Luis and Kayla's Learning Centers (cont'd)	
Learning Centers	Activities
Learning Center 8 (Located in Biology classroom)	Students work independently, in pairs, or as a group. Center is designed for research activities related to a problem-solving question or an expansion of the information concerning cell, their similarities, differences, and importance to living organisms. All students have computer access and are capable of independent work where they develop a line of inquiry and prepare a written report for delivery to the class.
Learning Center 9 (Located in Biology classroom)	Students work independently on research activities related to a problem-solving question or an expansion of the information concerning cells, their similarities, differences, and importance to living organisms. All students have computer access and are capable of independent work where they develop a line of inquiry and prepare a written report for delivery to the class.
Learning Center 10 (Located in the library)	Intended for research, problem-solving questions, and further inquiry. Students have access to computers for independent work as outlined and approved by the teacher.

therefore, Luis and Kayla will work out a detailed, numbered, and color-coded schedule. Also, after students are accustomed to the learning center routine, a few centers may become "activity stations" with specific tasks that some or all students may complete as an anchor activity.

Product Modification

For every unit in the study of biology, students keep a collection of their work assignments in a folder. After the assignments are graded, the students insert them in their work folders. Some assignments may be inserted in an electronic work folder because a number of the required tasks can be completed on the computer. Some students, such as Maria, will either record various assignments or seek assistance from another student in recording the work in a text format. Luis and Kayla will also have students take photos of the models they create, and either print these for their work folder or add them to their electronic work folder. Danny will include his IEP objectives checklist as well as other assignments that will be recorded for him personally or from group work. Each student's work folder will be reviewed by Luis and Kayla at least biweekly. Using student work folders and the rubrics they have developed for the various assignments at the learning centers, Luis and Kayla will discuss the work folder assignments with their students. Luis and Kayla will use a mini-conference format and give continuous feedback in writing and at these conferences. This is a routine that Luis established while teaching middle school Life Science. Most students are used to this routine assessment; however, Luis and Kayla will review and demonstrate the routine prior to beginning a unit. They will set clear expectations for student outcomes and will use rubrics that they will review with students before students begin working at a center or completing a specific assignment.

Luis and Kayla are aware of the diversity of their students' readiness and experiences with biology. They will provide a variety of formats for students to express their understanding of the concepts being taught and experienced at the learning centers through their products. Luis and Kayla will give students choices of how to show what they have learned. For example, depending on their readiness and preferences, students may demonstrate the types of cells through three-dimensional models, drawings, or labeling photos. Students may present their comparing and contrasting of the types of cells and their comparing of proteins, carbohydrates, lipids, and nucleic acids using various modes of expression (e.g., poster or videotaped oral presentation). Luis and Kayla are focused on helping all their students succeed in learning about cells. They will continually monitor student progress through pre-assessments, completed assignments, and mini-conferences. Also, Luis and Kayla's students' products will be assigned based on their students' identified objectives and on students' preferences of how they can show their understanding of the unit objectives.

Each of these teachers—Amanda, Luis, and Kayla—began the journey to establish a differentiated classroom by first examining the classroom as it currently existed, the curriculum (explicit, hidden, and absent), the learning profiles of their students, and the instructional procedures currently in use. These teachers then focused on what *all* students should know, what *most* students should know, and what *some* students should know. Each teacher envisioned the different paths that could bring students to the goal. Their planning processes reflected their students' readiness, interests, and learning profiles, and their instructional practices incorporate flexible grouping, student choice, and modification of content, process, and product. Their classrooms are rich with profound ideas relevant to their students' lives. All of these teachers believed that their efforts to meet the needs of all their students improved their practice with more students meeting success. Although their journey is far from over, they believe they are on the correct path to effectively differentiate instruction in an inclusive classroom. They also believe this way of teaching is what all educators should strive to do and one that enriches their lives as well as the students they teach.

References

Bartlett, L. D., Weisenstein, G. R., & Etscheidt, S. (2002). *Successful inclusion for educational leaders.* Upper Saddle River, NJ: Merrill.

Batzle, J. (1992). *Portfolio assessment and evaluation: Developing and using portfolios in the K-6 classroom.* Cypress, CA: Creative Teaching Press.

Bender, W. N. (2012). *Differentiating instruction for students with learning disabilities: New best practices for general and special educators* (3rd ed.). Thousand Oaks, CA: Corwin.

Bender, W. N., & Waller, L. B. (2011). *The teaching revolution: RTI, technology, and differentiation transform teaching for the 21st century.* Thousand Oaks, CA: Corwin.

Bennett, J. B. (2012). *Op-Ed: Differentiated instruction: Easier in theory than in practice.* Retrieved from http://patch.com/new-jersey/southorange/differentiated-instruction-easier-in-theory-than-in-practice

Bos, C. S., & Vaughn, S. (2015). *Strategies for teaching students with learning and behavior problems* (9th ed.). Boston, MA: Allyn & Bacon.

CAST. (2015). *About universal design for learning.* Retrieved from http://www.cast.org/our-work/about-udl.html#.VrjjIvkrKUl

Creighton Martin, C., & Hauth, C. (2015). *The survival guide for new special education teachers.* Arlington, VA: Council for Exceptional Children.

Dweck, C. (2000). *Self-theories: Their role in motivation, personality, and development.* Philadelphia, PA: Psychology Press.

Fogarty, R. J., & Pete, B. M. (2011). *Supporting differentiated instruction: A professional learning communities approach.* Bloomington, IN: Solution Tree.

Forest, M., & Lusthaus, E. (1989). Promoting educational equity for all students: Circles and MAPS. In S. Stainback, W. Stainback, & M. Forest (Eds.), *Educating all students in the mainstream of regular education* (pp. 43–47). Baltimore, MD: Brookes.

Foster, C. (2015). Differentiating without drowning. *ASCD Express, 10*(11). Retrieved from http://www.ascd.org/ascd-express/vol10/1011-foster.aspx

Gardner, H. (1983). *Frames of mind: The theory of multiple intelligences.* New York, NY: Basic Books.

Gardner, H. (1991). *The unschooled mind: How children think and how schools should teach.* New York, NY: Basic Books.

Gardner, H. (1993). *Multiple intelligences: The theory in practice.* New York, NY: Basic Books.

Gardner, H. (1999). *Intelligence reframed: Multiple intelligences for the 21st century.* New York, NY: Basic Books.

Gartin, B. C., Murdick, N. L., Imbeau, M., & Perner, D. E. (2002). *How to use differentiated instruction with students with developmental disabilities in the general education classroom.* Arlington, VA: Council for Exceptional Children.

Gould, A., & Vaughn, S. (2000). Planning for the inclusive classroom: Meeting the needs of diverse learners. *Catholic Education: A Journal of Inquiry and Practice, 3*, 363–374.

Gregory, G. H. (2003). *Differentiated instructional strategies in practice. Training, implementation, and supervision.* Thousand Oaks, CA: Corwin.

Hamre, B. K., Pianta, R. C., Burchinal, M., Field, S., LoCasale-Crouch, J., Downer, J. T., … Scott-Little, C. (2012). A course on effective teacher-child interactions: Effects on teacher beliefs, knowledge, and observed practice. *American Educational Research Journal, 49*(1), 88–123. doi:10.3102/0002831211434596

Hanson, H. M. (2015). *DI: Differentiated instruction: Enhancing teaching and learning.* Port Chester, NY: National Professional Resources.

Hart, L. S. (1999). *Human brain and human learning.* Kent, WA: Books for Education.

Hattie, J. (2009). *Visible learning: A synthesis of over 800 meta-analyses relating to achievement.* New York, NY: Routledge.

Hoover, J. J. (2009). *Differentiating learning differences from disabilities: Meeting diverse needs through multi-tiered response to intervention.* Upper Saddle River, NJ: Pearson.

Hoover, J. J., & Patton, J. R. (2004). Differentiating standards-based education for students with diverse needs. *Remedial and Special Education, 25*(2), 74–78. doi:10.1177/07419325040250020101

Hoover, J. J., & Patton, J. R. (2005). *Curriculum adaptations for students with learning and behavior problems: Differentiating instruction to meet diverse needs* (3rd ed.). Austin, TX: PRO-ED.

Hourcade, J. J., & Bauwens, J. (2003). *Cooperative teaching: Sharing the schoolhouse* (2nd ed.). Austin, TX: PRO-ED.

Hunter, M. (1971). *Teach to transfer: Theory into practice.* El Segundo, CA: TIP Publications.

Imhof, M., & Picard, C. (2009). Views on using portfolio in teacher education. *Teaching and Teacher Education, 25*, 149–154. doi:10.1016/j.tate.2008.08.001

Jackson, C., & Larkin, M. (2002). RUBRIC: Teaching students to use grading rubrics. *TEACHING Exceptional Children, 35*(1), 40–45.

Janney, R., & Snell, M. E. (2013). *Modifying schoolwork: Teachers' guides to inclusive practices* (3rd ed.). Baltimore, MD: Brookes.

Jensen, E. (1998). *Teaching with the brain in mind.* Alexandria, VA: ASCD.

Jensen, E. (2005). *Teaching with the brain in mind* (2nd ed.). Alexandria, VA: ASCD.

Kame'enui, E. J., & Simmons, D. C. (1999). *Toward successful inclusion of students with disabilities: The architecture of instruction. Volume 1: An overview of materials adaptation.* Reston, VA: Council for Exceptional Children.

Marilyn Friend, Inc. (2007). *Co-teaching approaches.* Retrieved from http://www.marilynfriend.com/approaches.htm

Mastropieri, M. A., & Scruggs, T. E. (2014). *The inclusive classroom: Strategies for effective instruction* (5th ed.). Boston, MA: Pearson.

Miller, S. P. (2002). *Validated practices for teaching students with diverse needs and abilities.* Boston, MA: Allyn & Bacon.

Nunley, K. (2006). *Differentiating the high school classroom.* Thousand Oaks, CA: Corwin.

Oliva, P. F., & Gordon, W. R. (2013). *Developing the curriculum* (8th ed.). Boston, MA: Pearson.

Ovando, C. J., Collier, V. P., & Combs, M. C. (2003). *Bilingual and ESL classrooms: Teaching in multicultural contexts.* Boston, MA: McGraw Hill.

Renzulli, J. S., Leppien, J. H., & Hays, T. S. (2000). *The multiple menu model: A practical guide for developing differentiated curriculum.* Mansfield Center, CT: Creative Learning Press.

Salend, S. J. (2011). *Creating inclusive classrooms: Effective and reflective practices* (7th ed.). Boston, MA: Pearson.

Schumm, J. S. (1999). *Adapting reading and math materials for the inclusive classroom.* Reston, VA: Council for Exceptional Children.

Schumm, J. S., Vaughn, S., & Harris, J. (1997). Pyramid power for collaborative planning. *TEACHING Exceptional Children, 29*(6), 62–66.

Schumm, J. S., Vaughn, S., & Leavell, A. G. (1994). Planning pyramid: A framework for planning for diverse students' needs during content instruction. *The Reading Teacher, 47*, 608–615.

Silver, H., Strong, R., & Perini, M. (2000). *So each may learn: Integrating learning styles and multiple intelligences.* Alexandria, VA: ASCD.

Simon, C. A. (n.d.). *Using the think-pair-share technique.* Retrieved from http://www.readwritethink.org/professional-development/strategy-guides/using-think-pair-share-30626.html

Sousa, D. A., & Tomlinson, C. A. (2011). *Differentiation and the brain: How neuroscience supports the learner-friendly classroom.* Bloomington, IN: Solution Tree.

Sternberg, R. (1985). *Beyond IQ: A triarchic theory of human intelligence.* New York, NY: Cambridge University.

Tomlinson, C. A. (1995). *How to differentiate instruction in mixed-ability classrooms.* Alexandria, VA: ASCD.

Tomlinson, C. A. (1999). *The differentiated classroom: Responding to the needs of all learners.* Alexandria, VA: ASCD.

Tomlinson, C. A. (2000). Reconcilable differences: Standards-based teaching and differentiation. *Educational Leadership, 58*(1), 6–11.

Tomlinson, C. A. (2001). *How to differentiate instruction in mixed-ability classrooms* (2nd ed.). Alexandria, VA: ASCD.

Tomlinson, C. A. (2014). *The differentiated classroom: Responding to the needs of all learners* (2nd ed.). Alexandria, VA: ASCD.

Tomlinson, C. A., & Allan, S. D. (2000). *Leadership for differentiating schools & classrooms.* Alexandria, VA: ASCD.

Tomlinson, C. A., Brighton, C., Hertberg, H., Callahan, C. M., Moon, T. R., Brimijoin, K., … Reynolds, T. (2003). Differentiating instruction in response to student readiness, interest, and learning profile in academically diverse classrooms: A review of literature. *Journal for the Education of the Gifted, 27*(2/3), 119–145.

Tomlinson, C. A., & Imbeau, M. B. (2010). *Leading and managing a differentiated classroom.* Alexandria, VA: ASCD.

Tomlinson, C. A., & Imbeau, M. B. (2013). Differentiating instruction. In D. R. Reutzel (Ed.), *Handbook of research-based practice in early education.* (pp. 119–139). New York, NY: Guilford.

Tomlinson, C. A., & McTighe, J. (2006). *Integrating differentiated instruction and understanding by design.* Alexandria, VA: ASCD.